# UNWAVERING PERSEVERANCE

# MARY WINEBERG

## AN OLYMPIC GOLD MEDALIST FINDS PEACE

outskirts
press

*For Athens,*
*You came into my life and made an ultimate influence.*
*You followed your heart and for this*
*I am thankful.*
*I love and miss you dearly and I know you will forever be*
*My Angel.*
*Lord, I will lift mine eyes to the hills*
*Knowing my help is coming from You*
*Your peace, You give me in time of the storm*
*You are the source of my strength*
*You are the strength of my life*
*I lift my hands in total praise to you*
*You are the source of my strength*
*You are the source of my life*
*I lift my hands in total praise to you!*
*This was one of your favorite songs*
*And I will forever remember it as YOU*
*-Total Praise (written by Richard Lee Smallwood)*

# Table of Contents

# Preface

We are born into this world and given a chance for greatness. We are born into this world and must find our own path to success. We are born to give and be our best. We are born to never give up! You must never give up hope. You can accomplish what you were born to do.

I challenge you all reading this book to never give up hope under any circumstance. Go after it, dream big, complete the challenge and make your own journey. I hope my story will not only allow you to embrace your shortcomings and downfalls, but also allow you to learn the ability to persevere and know that anything is possible! Writing this helped me to self-heal and I hope that reading it will help you also. No matter the struggles you may be going through or have gone through, you must find a way to forgive and forget. You should always try to find the good in people and not dwell on their flaws. This process has allowed me to be honest, shed tears, feel pain and move on with my head held high, ready to experience new relationships and new beginnings.

I hope that you are able to walk away feeling driven and ready to put your goals to the test. I pray that each and every one of you get the same strength and encouragement that I was blessed with to continue to be the best. My faith in the Lord has been the driving force in my life each and every day. I thank him for providing me with strength, encouragement and patience. There is hope in every situation. You must never accept that something is impossible. These quotes are favorites of mine and have inspired me to tell my story:

"There is no greater agony than bearing an untold story inside you"

"I can be changed by what happens to me. But I refuse to be reduced by it"

"We delight in the beauty of the butterfly, but rarely admit the changes it has gone through to achieve that beauty"

-All by the remarkable Maya Angelou

Would this little girl continue to grow in confusion and fall short, or would her new life allow her to reach her destiny? Would tragedy take her off course or actually propel her in the right direction? Would she learn to overcome struggles and setbacks or would she give up and accept that she was just average? Would the future allow her to seek her true reason for being on this earth? Read and see how this little girl overcame being a ward of the state with seemingly no hope for greatness, to make history in the world of sports and become an Olympic Gold Medalist.

# Acclamations

It has been a joy and privilege to be Mary's teammate over the years. She is a fierce competitor who possesses an amazing ability to encourage, uplift and motivate those around her. Mary's story is inspirational and it has been incredible to witness her success while making those around her better on the track, but more importantly in life.

*Allyson Felix,* the most decorated female Olympian in track and field history. She has won 9 Olympic medals and 16 World Championship medals.

How many women allow themselves to dream the dream of becoming an Olympic track and field champion? How many of those have the determination, perseverance, and drive to follow that dream to its fruition? Mary's is an uplifting story of a young girl from Brooklyn, N.Y., who did just that. Always the underdog, Mary had to struggle to win her opportunity to compete on the world stage. At the age of 28, Mary competed in the Beijing Olympics and won a gold medal in the women's 4x400 Relay. However, the True Jewels may be the experiences of the journey.

**Jim Schnur,** Coach of Mary Wineberg, former US ranked decathlete. NCAA Division I coach for over 20 years and University of Cincinnati Hall of Fame Inductee.

Mary Wineberg reminds me of a light in a dark tunnel that never goes out. She has overcome many obstacles in her life personally and athletically to blossom into a beautiful butterfly.

**Tyree Washington,** 400 meter track and field World Champion.

Traveling on this amazing journey to Olympic gold as my wife's training partner was an unbelievable experience. No personal accomplishment or achievement has been more satisfying or fulfilling than aiding in the success of my wife. Her story inspires and motivates me to always believe in the athletes I coach and that you can overcome any obstacle in life. I was happy to be her training partner and even more happy to be her partner in life.

**Chris Wineberg,** University of Cincinnati Track and Field Coach, NCAA All-American in the decathlon.

Beginning from her collegiate days of running, Mary demonstrated an incredible desire to train and dominate in the 400. Coupled with Mary's tenacious approach to competing, she has always displayed an uncommon level of grace, class and dignity, which now is even more impressive, as she reveals her deepest personal challenges in this book. This wonderful mix of athletic excellence and being a woman of character, explains why her teammates, both at the collegiate, national and global level, continue to have so much respect for her accomplishments, a journey culminating with her gold medal at the 2008 Olympics.

**Dr. Lewis Johnson,** 9-time Olympic broadcaster for NBC Sports and Olympics, University of Cincinnati Alum.

# Prologue

How did this young girl push through adversity, challenges, and despair? How will you relate to her story, how will you persevere to be your best? Will you see past her setbacks and see the beautiful gem that she has become? She battled with feeling abandoned, wanting to look a certain way, and ultimately making a name for herself in the prestigious world of track. Would marriage, motherhood and a career change allow her to grow even more? Would she be able to let go of those negative thoughts that tried to creep into her head. Would the tears of pain eventually turn into tears of joy? Read and see how you can help in turning your future into one that may be filled with peace.

# ONE

## Losing Him

If I were to look back at my life to when I was just four years old and try to imagine where it would ultimately lead, I would certainly not forecast that I'd be where I am today. I had never been exposed to death. Death to some is a word that not only invokes sadness, but also fear and despair. At this young age of four, I did not know what to feel or what to say as I stood staring at his body in the beautiful blue casket. He was dressed in a dark blue suit and I kept wondering "when would he open his eyes and call out my name?" When would things be back to how they were? Was he really gone? Yes, indeed that was the reality; he was really gone and there was nothing I could do to bring him back. There was nothing that this little girl whom he adored could do. Why, I thought, why did this have to happen? I loved him with all my heart and he was the best grandfather a girl could ask for, but now he was gone. I slowly leaned over the casket and for the last time kissed him gently on his cheek, whispering, "I love you." I walked away with the cold wet tears streaming down my face. I quickly ran to her arms and she hugged me close, telling me that everything would be okay. She told me that we would get through this. Death to me was a disappointment, it was unbelievable. It was my first crushing experience and it would never be forgotten.

Psalm 27:1-2

"The Lord is my light and my salvation. Whom shall I fear?
The Lord is the strength of my life. Of whom shall I be afraid?"

Leaving New York was such a big deal, and at the young age of four and a half, I wasn't prepared for it and did not know what it would entail. I wanted my grandfather back so badly, I continued to question why did this have to happen to him? Why didn't he get to say goodbye? I wanted to tell him so many things and give him the lovely picture I had drawn for him earlier in the day. I could recall the two of us walking the dog past our building steps, a daily activity, the sun shining brightly on our faces. And I recall hearing the buzzing of the cars driving down Sterling Street. This day would never be forgotten. It had started off well but would end in despair, losing a loved one and being at a complete loss for words.

I can recall that day so vividly...there were screams and more screams as the ambulance pulled away from the stoop of my apartment building on Sterling Street. The neighbors were out in front of the building; kids were playing but immediately stopped to see what was occurring. I remember being outside with some of the kids and having no worries. I was playing and having the time of my life. I had always played on the stoop of our building, and never would I have imagined this day to be so devastating. I didn't know what was going on! Athens, the lady I called grandmother, was overwhelmed with pain! The tears rolled down her cheeks and I could see a neighbor fanning her and holding her up. I knew that something was deeply wrong. I continued to observe and heard Athens scream out to one of the neighbors to watch over me. That meant it must be bad news! I thought to myself, what could have happened that was this bad? My sad little face could only try to imagine what was occurring and what was the cause of it. I was scared as I watched my grandmother ride away with the ambulance that carried my grandfather. All I could do is wonder. What just happened and when are they coming back? The neighbor continued to hold me and I can remember her saying that everything was going to be okay. I tried to believe her, but something inside me was telling me that everything was NOT okay. I was stunned and scared. I shook as she comforted me, but the wet, salty tears continued to roll down my face. I could not stop them. All I could think about was my grandmother and my grandfather. I wanted them both more than ever and I wanted them now.

Hours went by, but it felt like days! I can remember waiting and crying, asking when Athens would return. The neighbor stayed very calm and assured me that as soon as she was able to return she would. I could only sit and wonder. Several hours crawled by and I did not want to eat or play. I sat thinking of the man who they had taken out on the stretcher. All I could think about was him and the ambulance that drove away with him. The flashing lights, the loud sirens and the image of my grandfather--one of the nicest men I had known, the one that I looked up to. Again I wanted to know what happened, where was he and was he coming home that night? Finally, there was a soft knock on the door and in walked my grandmother. She looked exhausted, frail, and her eyes were bloodshot. I ran immediately to her arms and she just held me. She held me and didn't let go. Right there and then, I knew he wasn't coming back. Athens thanked the neighbor, they hugged, and we headed up the stairs to our front door. The neighbor knew that Athens needed her space and of course she needed to talk to me. She allowed us to leave in peace and reminded Athens that she would stop by to check on us in a few. My grandmother nodded her head and walked me up the stairs slowly. As Athens pulled out her keys, I could see her hands shaking and I just held onto her legs even tighter. We walked into our apartment and our dog stood at the door with a sad look on his face. Our German shepherd looked as if he knew his master would not be returning. My grandmother slowly fed him, sat at the table, and asked me to come over to her. I just stood there in shock and confusion and she knew I couldn't understand what was occurring. She calmly looked me in my eyes, and began to explain what had happened.

Again it hit me that my grandfather, Square would not be coming home. He didn't make it..... Yes he didn't make it. "How could this be?" was the thought running over and over in my little head. I had just seen him earlier that morning at breakfast. He not only looked fine, but was full of laughter, as we ate our Corn Flakes and drank orange juice together. This was one of our regular breakfast times in which I could spend time with him before he headed to work. My grandfather was a tall man and I could remember him sitting at the table with his legs stretched out and realizing that I wished I could be that tall when I grew up. He stood over six feet tall and was such a hard worker. He had worked for Con Edison, and was also known as the building supervisor for the apartment building in which we lived. My last memory of him that morning was of him sitting at the kitchen table in his uniform. I still didn't understand what was occurring as I held onto my grandmother's arms. Her mouth was moving, but I couldn't hear anything. Athens held me and didn't let me go. I could finally hear what she was saying, "He didn't make it; your grand-daddy isn't coming back." The tears swelled rapidly in my eyes, and one by one they fell and soaked my dress. This was the worst day of my life, the day that changed everything.

I now knew death and a little of what it entailed. It's interesting how losing a life can bring other lives closer! My grandmother and I held each other, and I must have fallen asleep because the next morning came quickly. I awoke to the sun shining brightly through the apartment window. I was hoping what occurred yesterday was just a bad dream. I immediately saw that it wasn't and again questioned the reason behind why it had to happen. The apartment was somewhat quiet. Athens and the dog were the only ones there, but they were moving around slowly.

I heard a knock on the door as I walked into the kitchen. One of my grandmother's close friends had come over to check on us. Her friend immediately hugged me and as I went to sit down to eat breakfast, my grandmother grabbed me again and hugged me tight. She gave me a big kiss and greeted me with, "Hey sweetie, how are you doing this morning?"

I wanted so badly to scream and say how I truly felt, but the voice inside me had rendered me mute. I felt something pressing so hard on my chest it hurt. I didn't know what it was at the time, but I would soon learn that it was the pain of losing a loved one. I could hear Athens and her friend discussing what to do next. Athens stated sadly that she needed to call the funeral home, the church, my grandfather's job and all our family members. She expressed that she didn't think that she would be strong enough to do it. She didn't know if she had the energy to do it, or the strength to make those calls. What and how would she tell everyone? No one is ever prepared for such a tragedy. Her voice sounded like it would crack at any time and she was constantly on the verge of tears. Her friend assured her that even in this time of despair God would never leave her side and that he would help her through this.

Psalm 33:4

"For the word of the Lord is right and true; he is faithful in all he does."

Deuteronomy 31:6

"Be strong and courageous. Do not be afraid or terrified because of them, for the Lord your God goes with you; he will never leave you nor forsake you."

She assured Athens that she would be there to help with anything that she needed. After they both shed some more tears, I remember seeing my grandmother wipe her face with tissues, murmuring, "I have to make sure that I have myself together for this little one. I don't want her to see me like this, not like this."

They both looked over at me, as I sat at the table and I wondered what would become of me. Where would I go since I had just lost my grandfather? I didn't want to lose her too. My grandfather had married Athens and she was not my biological grandmother. Would I be able to stay with her or would I have to leave? I heard Athens friend ask her, "Where is her mother, we have to let her know."

As I sat eating my cereal, the milk started to drip from the spoon making a small mess on the table. I heard my grandmother tell her friend that she would immediately try to contact my mom. I didn't know what would happen next. Could a blessing appear from such a sad, sad event?

While attending college, I learned an awesome poem that encouraged me to Never Quit! It entered my mind as I wrote this chapter. No one will ever realize just how hard it was to write and try to write daily, especially this first chapter. I told myself on so many occasions that I would write and finish this book quickly. I told myself that it wouldn't affect me, and I told myself that it would be easy, because I was just recalling memories. I was wrong and I was immediately reminded that sometimes even years later one isn't completely healed from such a tragedy.

It has been thirty-three years since I lost my grandfather. At the age of thirty-seven I did not think I would break down and cry as I did when I was four years old. Writing this chapter brought back so many memories. He was an angel for me and my protector. It was very hard to write down my feelings and to go back into time, and revisit that day of losing him. I still have Athens album in which she took pictures of her and Square's beautiful wedding day and at the end of that album are his funeral and gravesite pictures. For many years I could not bear to look at those pictures. I could not bear to see his face in that casket and be reminded that he was still gone and not coming back. Then as I continued writing, I immediately felt a sense of calmness and peace settle over me. I began to feel that he was so proud of what I have become. I now realize that he would never have wanted me to quit and for that reason I am such a hard worker today. I am truly at peace with his death. He is an angel looking down at me and I am his little princess who will never quit in Life! Here is a small excerpt from the poem:

> Success is failure turned inside out,
> The silver tint of clouds of doubt,
> And you can never tell how close you are,
> It may be near when it seems afar,
> So stick to the fight when you're hardest hit,
> It's when things seem worst that you must not QUIT.

-Edgar A. Guest

My days as a young child were different than most of my peers who had both parents involved in their lives. I had been living with Square, my grandfather, and my grandmother, Athens, since the age of two. Now that my grandfather had passed away following a massive heart attack, I was being raised by Athens. She was the lady I had known since I was born, who took me into her home at the young age of two, and who was willing to give me the best life that she could possibly give. She became my life savior and a blessing from God. I would later learn as an adult that Athens couldn't have children and she cared for me like I was her own, even after losing her husband and even though I wasn't hers. She still pushed forward and did what she had to do. My birth mother had me at the young age of sixteen and for her it may have been too much to care for me. She was still a child too. She loved me with all her heart, but did not know how to be a mom. My birth mother had lost her mother at the age of eighteen and this may have caused her to lose her way. I wonder if my mom was just mentally broken at losing her mother. Was it too much for her to handle?

I would not see my birth mother again for over thirty years.

So I'd lived with Square and Athens since I was two. Square, who was originally from Alabama, had married Athens, a lovely Jamaican woman with a spunky attitude and a strong accent. My birth mother would come and see me while I was ages two to four, but those visits became limited and then were eventually non-existent. Yes, life with my grandparents started off as a couple of days, but that turned to weeks and then months at a time that I would not see my mom. I became accustomed to living with them, I loved them dearly and it felt like home. I began to wonder if my mom really loved me and why I didn't live with her. I remembered my mother's voice and her face but soon those became fuzzy and slowly dissolved. Losing Square at four years of age was like an awful dream. Wake up, Mary, is what I tried to tell myself, wake up and everything will be back to normal. I imagined waking up to life as it was before—our routine of his arrival home from work, his familiar greeting, and taking the time to give me a big hug and kiss. I still can hear his strong husky voice and see his tall body come through the doorway as he reached over to pick me up, saying, "How is my little girl today?"

His smile and the pride were priceless. They shone through his eyes as he boosted me up into his arms. The smile that spread across my face communicated the same feeling---the feeling of love. He was definitely one proud grandfather. I actually found out thirty years later that Square wasn't my real grandfather. He had dated my birth mother's mom many years before he was married to Athens, and committed to helping take care of the kids that she had. He wanted to help out, and when I was born it excited him to help out even more. He wanted my birth mother to see that she could get back on track. He wanted her to see that she did have a life ahead of her that could become a positive one.

This was now reality and not a dream. Square was gone and what would we do? Where would we go and what would happen to me? The shock of everything was so numbing. Not only had my grandmother lost her husband but she had lost her friend. What she did next would forever change my life—this tragedy allowed Athens to make a decision to pursue her life elsewhere. Yes, she had had a life in Brooklyn, New York with Square for such a long time, but now that he was gone she felt the need to start over. She had no idea at first of where she was going. Would she go back to Jamaica to be with her brother and family, or head to Chicago to be with her sister and family? She also had family in Florida and Georgia. Square's family lived in Ohio, would she go there? She prayed that the Lord would give her guidance and clarity regarding what to do. It's interesting how the Lord works in mysterious ways; he answers when we least expect it. Athens battled with deciding to stay closer to her family in Chicago or to go to Cincinnati to see Square's family. She had no idea that this child she had been helping to care for would ultimately become her own and such a blessing. In this case, he allowed her to think clearly and come up with a plan. Athens boldly chose Cincinnati, Ohio; and this is where the new chapter of my life was about to unfold.

In preparing to move to Cincinnati, it was a struggle for Athens to locate my birth mother. As a child I didn't have very many memories of my birth mother because I didn't see her much. I do remember some things, but for the most part it is very vague. She had not been to visit me in weeks, but when it was time to move to Cincinnati, she arrived at our building in New York a couple days before. I can remember hearing her and Athens talk. My birth mother was in no way able to care for me. She was sixteen when she had me and now at twenty, she still did not have her life in order. She admitted that she needed to get herself together to be able to care for me in a safe way.

After a long discussion, she decided that she would let Athens take me to live with her in Cincinnati, but it was only supposed to be temporary, until she got things together. Yes, no mother ever wants to leave their child or hand them over to someone else to raise, trusting that this someone would make the right choices for them each and every day. My birth mother had made up her mind to let me go. It hurt her dearly and her family did not agree with her decision. With tears in her eyes she said her goodbye, promising to come get me as soon as she could. Athens reminded my birth mother that she could call and visit whenever she wanted. She also told her that she would never change her phone number. The only thing she needed to do was call the phone operator and she could even call collect to get through to us. All she had to do was give Athens first and last name and the operator would connect her to us immediately. I remember the last words out of her mouth, "Bye, Qwana baby, I will come get you soon."

What would Cincinnati, Ohio be like? Where would I live, where would I go to school, who would be my friends? I would be leaving behind a mother who gave birth to me, but also a side of her family I hardly knew. There had to be a reason why my life would be taking this course. Things always happen for a reason. This was to be a blessing in disguise. Athens had our things packed and we said our goodbyes to New York, the city that never sleeps.

# TWO

## The Move and Broken Promises

In 1984, we arrived in Cincinnati, Ohio to the open arms of family members from my grandfather's side of his family. They not only welcomed us, but consoled us, as they were mourning the loss of Square as well. I didn't remember this side of the family, but boy did they remember me. You see, previously, Square constantly bragged and bragged about me to his family. Mary this and little Mary that, ever since I was born. He adored me and believed that I was special. They told me about the time when I was two years old and Square had brought me to Cincinnati to visit with them. He took me on an airplane all by himself. Athens was invited, but decided to stay back in New York. My birth mother was going to come, but her fear of airplanes did not allow her to make the trip. Square took me with my bottles, diaper bag and all that I needed, and it was a successful trip. It is here that my Danner family got the chance to not only meet me but hold baby Mary. My grandfather's mother, sister, and brothers resided in Cincinnati, Ohio and it was quite interesting to hear about my first visit to their city.

Now that Cincinnati was going to be our home, the Danner family was happy to have me back. They hugged on us all day and night. I knew that we were in a place of love and understanding. The Danner family would make sure that Athens and I had a place to stay, food to eat and opportunities to make this new place into our home. At this moment I saw love and I was reminded that even though Athens wasn't my birth mother she would make sure that I was well taken care of.

We moved into a home that she was able to find and Athens was excited to get me enrolled in school. She made sure that she had everything in order so that I was well taken care of. She was a true definition of how hard work reaps huge benefits. She didn't depend on anyone to take care of her; she had the mentality that if you want something, then you need to work hard for it. I never thought of it until now but I was truly amazed at this woman, a single parent who made sure that I always had everything I needed. She was my everything and my blessing in disguise. She taught me so much during my young years and even beyond that. I am so thankful for having such an inspirational woman in my life. Not only did Athens serve as a mother to me, but she became my friend as I grew older. She did an awesome job in raising me to be the woman I am today.

While in Cincinnati, school years were great and I had no problem making friends. Although it was a new home, it was like I belonged there. I loved the house we moved into, which was in a neighborhood called Golf Manor. It was quiet, lots of green grass, trees, a backyard and a lot of things to do nearby. Our house was a two family home in which we lived on the top floor and rented out the bottom floor. Athens did not have an advanced education, but she was very wise and smart with money. She utilized the insurance money from my grandfather's death to purchase this home. Not only did she secure stable housing for us, but she generated a steady income as the landlord of this property. The neighborhood was very nice and the neighbors were welcoming. I was happy to be where we were and I felt safe, well taken care of and, most of all, at ease. Lying in my bed for the first time was so comforting and I felt a peace in this place, my new home. I was five years old now and my personality was beginning to blossom. I was getting taller and I was very social. This was me, a girl from New York who still had a little bit of an East Coast accent but fit in well in Cincinnati. I did eventually lose my accent, but will never forget my time in New York.

From age's five to eight, the calls from my birth mother became less and less frequent. I did not let it affect me; I pushed to work hard in school. My goal was to get good grades, make friends and have a great time learning all that I could. I became numb to the promises she would make and not keep. For a period, I didn't even care anymore that I wasn't living with her and rarely even questioned why. All I know is that she was wherever she was and I was here finding a new path for my life.

I remember when I was six years old and she called the operator and was connected to our number. She promised that she would come and get me for Thanksgiving and she would visit us for a while. You should have seen my face light up as I talked to her on the phone. I was so ecstatic; the smile that came across my face probably measured two feet wide. I had not seen this woman in two years and I missed her dearly. We talked for a little bit more on the phone, and I then handed the phone over to my grandmother. Athens spoke with her for a while, and caught up with her on her life and what was going on. I could tell that the conversation was productive and I saw Athens smile while on the phone with her. As they continued to talk, I played with my toys and I heard Athens give Corrine the address where we were living and all the necessary information on how to get to Cincinnati. Athens let her know when the Greyhound typically runs, the times and how long the trip would take. She further went on to tell Corrine that I really missed her and wanted to see her badly. As a little girl it was hard going to school and having people ask "Why don't you live with your mom? Where is she?"

I went through these types of questions for years and played it off as if it didn't affect me. Deep down inside it made me angry, it made me upset, it made me feel like I was missing something that others had. There was barely a day that went by that I did not ask about my birth mother. Athens would always say positive things to give me hope and not let me think I was abandoned. She would ease my heart and let me know that I was loved.

Thanksgiving of that year came and went. Christmas of that year came and went, and even New Year's, and there was still no visit from my mother. What had happened? I was not only devastated but heartbroken, because as a seven-year-old girl I was holding her to her promise of coming to see me or even get me. It was now my birth-day.........January 3rd.

After another no-show, I asked my grandmother why she did not come. I asked if it was because she didn't care about me anymore? I sat with the biggest scowl across my face and pouted the entire rest of the day. My grandmother assured me that my birth mother still loved me no matter her situation, and that she would always love me. She stated to me that maybe something happened or maybe she had to change her plans due to an unforeseen circumstance. Her explanation still did not take the pain away. I felt lonely even though I wasn't alone.

As the days went by, I'd get so excited whenever the phone rang, and think maybe it was her calling to say sorry. Maybe she was calling to explain herself or tell me that she was really coming this time. I never got that call I was looking for, but several weeks after my birthday, the phone rang and sure enough it was her on the phone. My eyes lit up and I ran to the phone and immediately said, "Mommy.... why didn't you come?"

She didn't have an answer and just said some things had come up. She said that she wasn't able to call and that she wasn't able to come visit. I talked with her for a few more minutes, and she swore that she would come visit just as soon as possible. I had the biggest smile on my face and I told her that I would like that! I couldn't wait to see her. It had been years and I didn't remember what she looked like. I wondered if she remembered what I'd looked like, even though I was as tall as a broomstick now! I was no longer that baby she had last seen in 1984, but a young girl who was taking on the world. We said our goodbyes and I was so excited that she said she would come see me soon.

My birth mother once again led me to believe that she was coming for me, but unfortunately that did not happen. Athens never wanted to see my heart broken time after time again. She tried her best to shelter me from many things, and she vowed that she would never talk badly about my birth mother. Athens was my backbone and I admired the fact that she was a kind and nice lady who loved deeply. She was strict through the years, but went by the book and was fair. She always tried to assure me that my birth mother was just trying to get herself into a better place. She was trying to put herself in a position in which she could eventually come back and get me. I really wanted to believe that and all the promises that she made, but after many years went by I started to gain a type of feeling toward her—the type of feeling you get when you are annoyed, angry and most of all let down. A young child should never have to encounter this but I did--It happened to me. I secretly dealt with it, and there were many times in which I would just go to my room. I would lie on my bed or sit on my floor and cry it out. If Athens walked in, I quickly dried my tears and made it seem as if nothing had happened. I was good at making a wall and I had built it high so it wouldn't show my emotions when it came to my birth mother.

Two years later the phone rang and it was a collect call from New York. I answered the phone and I knew I had heard that voice before. It sounded familiar. I wasn't exactly sure and with an uncertain look upon my face I wanted to hand the phone off to Athens. The person kept saying, "It's me, your mom...." and I quickly handed the phone over. I don't know why I did what I did next but I immediately burst into tears and ran out of the room, screaming that I did not want to talk to her.

My grandmother picked up the phone just as I slammed the door of my room. I couldn't do it, I couldn't take anymore disappointments. Year after year, holiday after holiday, birthday after birthday, and this time I just couldn't take it! I really couldn't take it anymore! When Athens took the phone, I could see the upset look on her face and she too was surprised. She calmly said hello, and began to explain to my birth mother just what was happening with me. She explained that I was crying hysterically and the reason behind it all is that she was doing a number on me. She told my birth mother that if she couldn't make things happen or come and see her daughter then to stop making promises to such a young child. (Eight years old to be exact, and feeling helpless and lost). I now know that I'd begun to have separation issues, but didn't know it at the time. They continued their conversation and I heard Athens ask her where she had been all this time? My birth mother gave several excuses, none of them strong enough to support the pain that she had indeed put me through. Athens, too, could not take it anymore and she gave her a piece of her mind! She screamed into the phone, "Look, get yourself together, Mary will always be here and she will always be well taken care of. I promise you that! I am not going anywhere. We will always live in this house on Yosemite Drive right here in Cincinnati, Ohio. My number will never change and I will never change it because I want you to always be able to get in touch with Mary and have our number. If you ever lose the number you know that you can call collect and go through the operator. They will connect you at any time, day or night!"

"But you have to stop doing this to her; she can't possibly take anymore!"

This was my breaking point. The point when I realized that the lady I knew who gave birth to me was not in a position to make a life for me. She was not able to care for me and God had put someone else into place to serve as that vessel. I realized that I could not let it hurt me anymore. I could not let it determine who and what Mary would become.

# THREE

## A New Life for Me

After that phone call, I can say I became a slightly different little girl. I wasn't going to cry anymore about my situation or my past. I was only going to look forward from now on. I was still a very sensitive girl, but there would be no more tears as it related to my birth mother. I told myself that I was going to continue to enjoy my new neighborhood, school, and family. Athens continued to work hard each day to provide for us as an in-home provider. This gave her the opportunity to send me off to school each and every day.

She literally walked me to the bus stop every morning and waited until the bus came each afternoon. She did this until I was in high school. I often wondered why, and I felt embarrassed that this woman would be so adamant about making sure I got on the bus. Did she not trust me? I had never given her reason not to, but I realized it was a mother's love, a mother's duty and that is why she did it. She cared that much for and about me that she was making sure that I was safe and no one would harm me. I get it. She was being slightly overprotective, but she loved me dearly. My grandmother, as I referred to her, was the best. She went through these years as I continued to grow and made sure that I participated in all types of activities year round. She never wanted me to have to beg, feel a lack of and steal anything. She didn't spoil me, but she guided me to know the difference between wants and needs. I admired her for her strength and the ability to be a strong black woman caring for a young child by herself.

I did well in school. I attended Losantiville Elementary from 1985-1992 and enjoyed these years. My teachers allowed me to realize that I too wanted to be a teacher. I played the recorder, the flute and then the clarinet. I tried out for plays and even got involved in clubs and activities. My teachers guided me, cared for me, taught me well and allowed me to prosper. While in school, I used to talk so much, I would often get in trouble and that was one of my downfalls. The school occasionally had to call home because I was talking too much in class. They said I had a sweet little voice, but I wanted to use it a bit too much. Perhaps those years may have been giving me practice for becoming a future speaker and a teacher.

Some of the teachers I can remember include Mrs. Mallin, my Kindergarten teacher whom I adored. She was my first teacher and I wanted to not only please her, but also be one of her best students. Through the years, some of the other teachers I remember are Mrs. Burrell, Mrs. Cowit, and Mrs. Danner (who by the way was not related to me). We shared the same last name and I thought that was the coolest thing ever. I can remember my teachers so well based on the things they used to say and do. I remember the way Mrs. Cowit would walk into class, the way she said good morning to us and even the way she dressed. Such a classy lady and I wanted to be a great teacher like her.

I also enjoyed meeting my friends from Losantiville Elementary School. It was great to grow up with them. Many of them have gone on to do some amazing things. I can still remember how I met my best friend at Losantiville. I was very nervous about saying hi because she was the cool girl and the girl that everyone wanted to be friends with. Everyone loved Arrin and she was such a sweet and nice girl. I am happy that we grew closer and closer through the years. Growing up during these years, I didn't think about what and who I would become.

I just enjoyed the innocent years of being a child. There are so many experiences and individuals that made an impact on my life: things such as field day at school, bike riding through the streets of Golf Manor, blowing bubbles, walking the neighborhood, going to the corner store, hanging out with my friends on Ridgeacres, attending the Melrose YMCA, and establishing my spiritual background at Bethel Baptist Church.

I was truly blessed that Athens was able to give me a great childhood. I loved being involved in things that kept me busy each day. I loved to sing in the church choir. I may not have had the greatest voice, but I made a joyful noise. I also loved it when the pastor had children's church and all the kids headed to the steps to hear his message. The lessons learned from him helped guide me through the years.

While growing up, Athens made sure that I was at church every Sunday and on time for Sunday School as well. These were vital years as I found a relationship with God, accepted him as my Savior and wanted to live by his words. I enjoyed being surrounded by the other youth in my church. It is so amazing to see what some of us became. Gospel singers, pastors, lawyers, TV personalities, Olympic medalists all came out of this small African American Baptist church. I especially enjoyed the older folks at church. During my years of growing up we were taught to have the utmost respect for our elders and, boy, you had better show it or else. There wasn't a moment that went by that you did not greet an elder, give your seat up, help them carry things into church, and hug them every time you saw them. These influential older adults played a huge role in my life, served as mentors, and taught me how to be respectful.

Athens was a strict mother—one who was old school with strong Jamaican values. She was older than most of my friends' mothers and I would wonder if others noticed the age gap. I really enjoyed it when Athens side of the family would come and visit us. They were so much fun, so family-oriented, and the food would always be on point. Our fellowship with each other was beyond amazing and I never wanted it to end. I was able to experience Jamaican patties, red beans and rice, stew chicken, curry goat, plantains, coconut cakes, rum cake, snapper, boiled banana, akee, and, my favorite, jerk chicken.

There was one thing that I was not a fan of at first. Athens favorite thing to give me to drink was Classic Ovaltine. I didn't know why I couldn't just have Nestle like my friends, but I learned to love it.

I loved getting to know my Jamaican family. I enjoyed seeing my cousins grow, having my aunts and uncles encourage me, riding bikes through the streets of the neighborhood, and our strange tradition each year of seeing who can be pushed into the sticker bush that sat in front of my house. During holidays, I vividly remember either having our Jamaican family visit from Chicago or Georgia or going there to visit them. I was always sad when it was time for them to leave because that meant a much quieter house, no more Jamaican Patwa being spoken, and an end to their amazing storytelling. To this day, I love them with all my heart and enjoy the time we spend together. They never once made me feel as if I wasn't one of them. They took me into the family with loving arms, gave me guidance, and continue to be such a huge support. They treated me just like a Hepburn!! This family is my family! I am so honored to have them in my life. They are the greatest family one could ask for.

My personality as a child included being determined, sensitive, and very social. I loved to talk and was the opposite of shy. I also had a keen sense of direction. If I was riding in a car, I could easily remember the directions and could navigate the driver back to my house with no help. I also loved to read while growing up, and this would end up continuing to be one of my passions to this day. Nothing about me seemed exceptional and I had no idea I would accomplish something great as an adult. I was taller than most, very skinny, had long legs and arms, and didn't know that I was athletic.

The way I looked and felt would turn into an issue as I encountered puberty and my high school years.

I was called ET fingers, or described as lanky, long arms, skinny as a toothpick, too tall, and was picked on when I wore pants that were too short. During those years it was a struggle to find long enough jeans that would fit me. All of my pants were high water pants. I can remember coming home and being sad that someone had told me that my arms were too long and that I looked weird. I was told that I was too skinny and at the time I blew it off. In my high school years, the continued comments started to affect me. It made me think I wasn't pretty. It made me think that I wanted to look different, to be shorter and it made me wonder how I could change my appearance. I often looked at myself in the mirror and saw a young girl whose hair wasn't long enough, skin wasn't pretty enough and whose body looked too long. If my arms, my legs and my fingers could be shorter, that would be my wish.

It's interesting how kids can be cruel and not think about what they say and how it can affect others in the long run. Athens reminded me constantly that I was the best child anyone could ask for. She reminded me that my height was a beautiful thing and it was okay to be as thin as I was. God had made me exactly how he wanted me! I would eventually learn to love my appearance, my body, and realize that I was beautiful no matter what anyone says. Athens did a great job of keeping me involved in activities that kept me grounded and helped boost my confidence. I participated in Sunday School, Vacation Bible School, Children's Church, Guild Girls, Girl Scouts, summer camp, and had fantastic godparents and a god sister to help guide me. My godparents and god sister were amazing role models and I was thankful for their interest in me and all the help they provided through the years. Even though Athens was a single mom, she still had people to help her out if she needed anything along the way. She had my uncle, aunts, and cousins that were here in Cincinnati.

My Uncle Tommy, who was Square's brother, played a huge role in serving as my father figure. He always made sure that the Danner family connected through the holiday barbeques and he loved to sing in church. He was a great man and so wise! I wish he was still here today to see who and what this girl turned into. Family is important in that they guide you, protect you, encourage you and teach you the ways of the world. I had my Danner, Hepburn and Houston family!

Every Sunday night, Athens and I would read the Bible. The goal was to get through the whole Bible each year, discuss the events, and talk about what they meant. This was a bonding time for us. I questioned why we had to do this every Sunday, but I later realized its importance and cherished this ritual that Athens had started with me.

One night when I was twelve, I can remember looking at Athens as she read the Bible, and I quietly called her name. She immediately looked up and said, "Yes, Mary."

I don't know why I was so nervous to speak and say what was on my mind, but I slowly got the words to come out of my mouth. "Grandma, can I call you my mom?"

She looked startled and I could tell I had hit a sensitive subject. She slowly grinned from ear to ear and spoke the best words I could have heard. "Sure...you know you are my heart, I do everything for you and I would be honored!"

I did not know what needed to be done to allow Athens to become my mother but I was sure that she would look into it. Wow, I had gone through so many years of not being able to call anyone Mom. A simple three-letter word, but so important for a young girl. I was so happy and so excited. I could not wait to hear what the next steps were for Athens to officially become my mom. I was ready for this new chapter in my life. I wanted a mom just like my friends had. I physically had someone who was caring for me and providing for me and acting as my mom. I wanted it to be official. I was blessed to have such a dedicated person and a person who depended on the Lord daily to raise me. Athens prayed and asked the Lord to provide her with a solution and way to make this work for us. I knew that our prayers would be answered, I just didn't know how.

# FOUR

## Taking a New Name

The next morning I could see that we both had smiles and were full of laughter. I sat at the kitchen table watching Athens make breakfast and couldn't help asking a million and one questions: How would I explain to everyone my good news, my friends, my teachers, my church? Would I feel weird saying Mom instead of Grandma? Would people think that she was too old to be my mom? What would it feel like for her?

Athens contacted a lawyer here in Cincinnati and also talked to several social workers and lawyers back in Brooklyn, New York. She wanted to figure out if she could legally adopt me and if it was the right thing to do. She did not want to upset anyone, including my birth mother. Athens called and called, talked and talked for what seemed like a week straight on the phone. I can remember coming home from school each day and she would still be on the phone. This particular day she was on the phone with the Social Security Office trying to locate my birth mother.

Her close friend, Ms. Parker, beeped in on the other line. Athens took the call after finding out from the Social Security Office that they were unable to give any information to her regarding my birth mother. Ms. Parker was a friend that Athens had gotten to know through her years in New York. She was a sweet older lady who I remember as being very wise. I had learned that you never interrupt adults while they are on the phone. I heard them talking and I remember walking in and seeing the intensity on Athens face. She still had her strong Jamaican accent and if she got mad or upset, you could hear the feisty accent come out even more. I sat at the dining room table and tried to go on with my daily after-school routine, but I wondered what could be happening or was about to happen. I waited to say hello but it seemed like a deep conversation was occurring. Athens then hung up the phone and we quickly greeted each other as she sat down and sighed. In my mind I'm thinking 'Oh no, someone must be sick or something bad has happened.'

Athens looked at me and said, "Well, I talked with the lawyers and child welfare agency from New York. I have some good news and some bad news."

I eyed her with a confused look and wondered what might possibly be about to come out of her mouth. She first told me the good news: she could officially adopt me. "Your case has been reviewed by social services and has placed you as a ward of the State of New York."

I was very confused now, because I did not know what those words meant, ward of the state, or even social services. Athens quickly noticed my confused look and slowed down to explain. "Your birth mother has not been in the picture for a while now and the state of New York has also been looking to locate her for the past two months or more. Her numbers on file, past addresses, etc. are not producing anything or any way for them to contact her. The lawyers have advised me that due to the court's decision of me already being your legal guardian, I can now officially adopt you. I was just telling Mrs. Parker the news and she was so happy that this drawn out process is finally over."

I jumped up and down, hugging Athens, tears spilling from my eyes with happiness, while also feeling a tinge of guilt deep inside.

Wow, I was going to officially have her last name and be a Danner. I was going to have a new life. I wondered about my birth mother. What had happened to her?

The next morning I had to meet with several individuals regarding our case. We went downtown to the Cincinnati courthouse and I didn't know what to expect. Lawyers and social workers questioned Athens and they also questioned me. At the end of it all, Athens was officially able to adopt me, this young girl. All the girl had ever wanted in life was to see some kind of normal and be loved. I wanted to be able to say, "Hey, this is my mom," or call out Mom, instead of Grandma. I was so excited. Mary Shaqwana Wright would now be known as Mary Shaqwana Danner. Yes, my name would be changing but my past would still be a memory, and my present actions would help aid me for the future.

There was to be a big celebration and Athens planned a huge party to announce my adoption. She decided to invite all of our close friends, family, teachers, mentors and church family. I felt so special and I was in amazement at all the people we had in our lives that were so supportive. These individuals to this day continue to be so instrumental in my life, or have at least left lasting pieces of wisdom and memories. These are the kind of people I enjoyed having in my circle, in my life—just knowing that I could depend on them was wonderful. The day of the celebration was amazing, I got to dress up and my pastor from my church said some uplifting and encouraging words. Family members also came up to speak. Athens spoke about how happy she was to have been able to care for me and now to call me her daughter. I was on top of the world that day! Love was overflowing throughout the banquet hall and I can honestly say that God was in my corner, and he knew all along from the day I was born the life he was going to bestow on me.

Proverbs 3: 5-6

"Trust in the Lord with all your heart and lean not on your own understandings; in all your ways submit to him, and he will make your paths straight."

I was on cloud nine for days and months after the adoption celebration. I did have to adjust to writing a new name and got tired of explaining to my friends from school why my name had changed. At times it was funny to see the look on their faces, and then I finally reached a point where I stopped explaining. It wasn't because I was embarrassed. I was kind of tired of saying the same thing over and over again. Athens continued to be a great and awesome parent as I progressed into junior high and high school. She now got to experience having a teenager in the house. I remember that we had some good days and some hard days. As a teen you think you are always right, and it's hard for you to see things for what they are sometimes. But all in all we survived. We made it and I learned so much.

# FIVE

## High School Sports

The years had finally come for this little girl to step out of her comfort zone and seek out participating in sports and see where it would take her. In the 7th grade as I attended Walnut Hills I had a mild interest in sports, and I mean a really mild interest. Now don't get me wrong. I had always enjoyed running around the neighborhood or participating at Field Day at Losantiville Elementary, but to be on a team, that was kind of a scary thought for me. Athens also didn't fully understand the American school sports system. As a Jamaican in her hometown of Montego Bay, the kids played cricket and football, known here as soccer. The kids did these sports for fun after school hours and in the summer, but not for a school team. I can remember talking to my best friend, Arrin, and she had been running track for a while. She was going to try out for the junior high team. She suggested that I go to the tryouts and she let me know that it would be a lot of fun. I thought of this opportunity and I didn't see the fun of running at first, but I figured if I didn't fully enjoy it, it could serve as a social group to be a part of. There would be plenty of other boys and girls to meet, and if I made the team, I would have an opportunity to make a lot more friends. I was very excited to come home from school and tell Athens that I had a new interest–trying out for the junior high track team. She wasn't a huge fan of this and really pushed hard for me to just focus on my academics. She didn't understand what it meant to be on a track team, the practice and all that it entailed. She saw school as an opportunity to improve and set up for the future. School would allow me to go for my dreams and my profession. Athens just didn't think track would be a vital part, but later it actually became one of my stepping stones in life, allowing this butterfly to spread her wings and fly.

"Until you spread your wings you will have no idea how far you can fly" - Unknown

I was sad when Athens said no to my participation on the track team. I think she just needed a little persuasion. I finally had to have my best friend's mother talk to my mom and from there she lightened up. I was able to join the team and I was so excited. During my junior high years, I did indeed realize that I had some talent. I was one of the tallest in my grade and had the legs of a runner. What I once viewed as a negative attribute, was actually now a benefit! Coach Scottie and many of my teammates were amazing people to have met. I was able to learn about running, teamwork, character building and that playing sports could be fun and educational. I am amazed at the relationships that I still have to this day among the individuals with whom I ran junior high track. As I moved on to run in high school and was trained by Coach Karl he too saw something in me. I learned more and more fundamentals of running and it was an awesome opportunity to be coached by him. Those high school track years went by so fast! The memories of running in meets at Anderson High School were amazing, and most of all getting the chance to run the relays with my friends. Through running track I was also able to meet my other best friend, Autumn, who was very good at track. We would be known in our high school as the Track Thugs, which included Arrin, Autumn and myself and, of course, our other best friend, Eboni, who did not run track. These ladies were great to get to know and I was so happy to call them my friends.

No, we were not thugs, but we did perform in a talent show and made up our own raps. Here our goofy name originated. It was quite hilarious and still to this day we get called "Track Thugs" when we all are together. Track was the social group that I was hoping for but running became very important. I had acquired this new love for track and I was willing to work hard and dedicate myself to improving. In high school, my teammates made these some of the best years of my life—the stories we had, the fun and all the experiences! I thank you all for the fun times we had together. I have great memories of the bus rides, the practices, and having the support of my teammates. I became more secure with myself as an athlete, student, person, and as a young black girl who could learn to love the way she looked. I got over the fact that people would say that I was so tall. I got over being called lanky and I learned to use it to the best of my advantage. I enjoyed Walnut Hills and the top notch education I received. Walnut Hills was a CPS school and a great one at that. Through the years I admired the teachers and staff in making my years ones to be remembered. I was academically challenged and they prepared me for the college years that I would soon be approaching.

My long legs were an advantage, but I was not a star on the track at this point. I still needed to develop my skills and improve my times if I wanted to pursue track in college. Athens main concern was to make sure that I got my college education. She was willing to sacrifice in any way necessary to make sure I had the money to attend college. Athens did not have a higher education and my birth mother did not finish high school. I would be the first in my biological family to attend college. I can remember considering running track in college, but it wasn't a major priority. After discussing things with my mom, and then my coach, we came to the conclusion that I would probably stay in the city to attend school. I wasn't highly recruited because I had not run the times that were required to be considered a top recruit. Athens was a type 1 diabetic and through the years I felt that I needed to be super close to her just in case she had an episode of low blood sugar. These low blood sugar episodes happened more often than we would have liked for them to occur. At any given time, Athens could quickly deepen into a diabetic coma or pass out due to her low blood sugar. I made it my responsibility and passion to attend all her doctor's appointments and to make sure we both knew her signs/symptoms and what could be done immediately to help her. Yes, those moments were scary but as a determined girl I was fine with making sure she was ok and had someone in her corner. We depended on each other. She was a godsend to me and I was a godsend to her.

My teammates were being recruited for track and one of my best friends got a scholarship offer to Vanderbilt. We were excited for her. Now, I had to figure out what school I would attend. I was an average athlete, but I had hope and desire. I made it to the state meet in both the 4x200m relay and the 400 meters my senior year, but I did not advance to the state meet final in the 400 meters. My best time coming out of high school would end up being 57.80. I looked into a couple of schools and once I realized that I would be staying in the city my two options were the University of Cincinnati and Xavier University. Yes, I was considering a school which at the time in 1998 did not have a track program. I saw this vision of me being accepted into the school and going to the athletic department to discuss how a women's track and field program could be started. I even considered not running track and just pursuing my degree at Xavier. I still had an interest in attending UC, but had no idea what I needed to do to join the team. I had tentatively decided to attend Xavier, but the coaches from the University of Cincinnati saw me run at the state meet and invited me to come in for a visit. We met the coaches in their office: Carolye, Jim, and Bill. They were all very kind and I can remember the conversations that my mom had with them when they mentioned offering me a scholarship to attend to their school. At first she didn't understand that you could get an athletic scholarship, but the coaches clearly explained how it would work. We left the visit confident in knowing that I would be well taken care of at UC. I committed and I was going to be a Bearcat. I was so excited but I could never imagine all the things that would happen next.

# SIX

## Finding Courage and Believing in Myself

Athens was coping with her diabetes, but continued to have struggles while I was in college. She had to really monitor her blood sugar and watch her diet so that she would not pass out. I knew if I called her and she didn't pick up by the third ring something was wrong. I would immediately jump into my car, rush over from my dorm room and make the 12-15 minute drive to my childhood home in Golf Manor. During these episodes, she would be disoriented, seem disconnected and unable to state what was wrong with her. I would quickly give her some juice or a soft piece of candy to raise her blood sugar. This usually worked and she was back to herself in minutes. On other occasions, I didn't like that I had to call 911. The paramedics would come and have to inject her with medicine to quickly get her out of her diabetic stage. This was scary because I didn't want to lose her and I didn't want her to see how afraid I was. I tried very hard to stay strong in these situations. Just having to see your mom laid out and not able to help herself was very traumatic. Athens knew that she would have to seek out further help from her doctors in order to maintain appropriate levels for her blood sugars. She wanted to lower the occurrences and I wanted to feel confident that she was safe. In the end I was so thankful that I could be there for her.

College was to a good start, there were some hip-cups, but I was learning so much. I was living on campus and visiting home every weekend when I was not traveling for track meets. Athens would attend my home meets and invite my godparents, god sister, church members and other family members to attend. I had so many people supporting and believing in me. My god sister was someone that I looked up to. She was smart, independent and I wanted to be like her when I grew up. She always was checking in on me, giving me great advice and really being that sister that I never had. It felt great to have so many people in my corner and all of the support, but what many didn't seem to know was that I was battling with knowing how to properly believe in myself. The effects of being told in high school that I wasn't pretty enough, or too tall or just lanky continued on with me into college. I feared reaching my potential and I feared believing in myself. I finally realized toward my senior year in college that I did not believe completely in myself. I did not think that Mary could do it and I did not think I was good enough. I battled with self-esteem and put up a big front to the ones closest to me so they would think I was okay. I didn't show any signs of this on the surface and I acted as if I was a very confident person. My college friends probably would have said at this time that I was a silly, funny, and an enjoyable girl to hang out with.

Attending college and participating in sports was a huge and dramatic change for me. I had to take it day by day so as not to become overwhelmed, or wrapped up in the wrong things and live my life too freely. I was coming from a home in which my strict Jamaican mother did not play when it came to disrespect, lying, cursing, and doing things I had no business doing. I certainly made some mistakes, but also learned from them. My first year on the track team was an interesting one. I had left high school running 57.80 and first year at UC

I brought my time down to 55 seconds in the 400 meters. You might think, wow that is amazing and this girl should have nothing to complain about. Yes, I was proud of what I had done my freshman year in college, but I was not satisfied with who I was at the time. I had grown and found who I thought Mary was, but even then I was not certain. I wanted to be the best that I could be on the track. I wanted my teammates to like me and enjoy our times together. I wanted to excel in school and to make my mom proud. I realized that I needed to be more focused and couldn't party as friends did that were not committed to an athletic team. Yes, Athens was not there to watch me so I needed to watch myself and make sure that I was doing what I needed to do. She did threaten that she could pop up at my dorm room at any moment. I took that seriously and knew she meant business. Athens didn't play.

As I continued to compete in track, I found that I was comfortable in practice, at home meets, and at smaller competitions where I knew I could easily win. When I had to prove myself or race against better competition from around the region, here is where I doubted myself and would shatter into a million pieces. Who would have known that Mary Danner, the girl who put on the tough face, was really timid at big meets, afraid to succeed and afraid to fail. Jim Schnur was my coach through my junior year, and if you asked him, he probably would have said that I was a negotiator. I was constantly trying to change the workouts to make them easier. Jim was such a pleasure to have as a coach because he was so knowledgeable. He not only coached the sprints, but he also coached the heptathletes and decathletes. I can remember my roommate and I always trying to get out of doing the set number of repeat 200's or a repeat 150's, and trying to justify to Coach Jim why we deserved to cut off the last rep. Jim believed in me and wanted me to be my best. I truly wanted to end my Bearcat year on top, but I probably wasn't putting in the work to accomplish it.

I was pursuing a Health Promotions major out of the College of Education and I enjoyed my professors, other students that I had met, and the remainder of the college experience. I had even joined the prestigious Alpha Kappa Alpha Sorority, Incorporated in 2001 and here the young ladies I encountered and got to know so well, allowed me to flourish in character, beliefs, morals and developing more as a young lady. I enjoyed my line sisters and we were committed to doing service within our community. We gave back and I continued to mature as a person, learning to appreciate that I was an athlete and student. I learned to manage my time to ensure that I got good grades and stayed focused. I came into my own during those years and I became a confident young lady outside of track. I had made a great deal of progress, but I still wasn't 100 percent there when it came to my sport. I began to see myself as beautiful and I began to see my height and length as one of the greatest assets that I could own. I was thankful for how God made me and I wasn't going to let anyone tell me that I wasn't beautiful.

I also got the opportunity through these years to meet a wonderful man who I never thought would walk or should I say run into my life. He was first my teammate–someone I barely talked to and had no interest in. We were actually on the team for a full year together before we ever talked. When the timing is right, God makes things happen for a reason and opens your eyes to see things that you couldn't see before. One day on the track, I was running a cool down lap with a couple of my teammates, Charlyn and Shanekqua. They were not only great friends, but I learned so much from these ladies through our college years. As we jogged around the track, I mentioned to them that this guy looked kind of cute, but I was too afraid to approach him. My friends egged me on and said, "You'd better go and talk to him." I had just broken up with a guy who I can honestly say wasn't a good fit for me. My mother had tried to warn me about him, but I was too stubborn and had to realize it on my own. It later kicked me in the bottom as I saw that he was not the guy God wanted me to have in my life. I quickly got over the guy and seeing this teammate of mine actually brought a sense of happiness to me in words that I can't describe. I was nervous and scared because I did not want to be rejected. I knew that we had great differences and I wasn't quite sure what his reaction would be to me. I was a brown skinned girl and I was sort of goofy. I first approached him with the line of, "I know someone who likes you." That was the pickup line......I guess he was impressed!

I was hoping for the best and the best did come. We started dating shortly after I wowed him with my pickup line and I was on cloud nine. Had I found my soulmate? We did indeed end up having so many things in common and what I feared the most actually turned out not to be that big of a deal. Black, white...it didn't matter to him and it didn't matter to me. We liked each other for who we were and what we were about. Even though Chris was a white male and I was a black female, we didn't let that stop us from being together. My sorority sisters were actually very supportive and liked him. I was relieved to find out how welcoming they were to Chris. Athens absolutely adored him and I was happy that his parents liked me too. Our relationship continued to blossom through the rest of our college years and we supported each other on and off the track.

Entering my senior year, I wanted to be the best in the 400 meters! The season was going well and everything led up to our last meet of the season, the Conference Championship Meet. Chris was a phenomenal athlete. At the conference meet, he competed in the decathlon which includes ten events and he also did the open pole vault, open javelin and ran on the 4x400 meters relay. I had picked a stud! He ended up placing in every event that year. I went into the meet and my body felt pretty good. My previous injuries weren't acting up and I was super nervous. I was nervous because this was a big stage for me. No more small meets, or running against the same competitors that I saw from week to week. This was a different track and a different stage. This was one of the meets where all the athletes came to shine. I can remember warming up and seeing all of my competitors. We all were doing the same drills and the same exercises. I remembered some of the 400 meter girls from the Indoor Conference Meet that year and I was going to have to run my best to place. I remember seeing other runners from Tulane, Houston, Louisville, and South Florida. What was I going to do?

During the warm up, my roommate and teammate, Charlyn, saw that something was wrong. She knew me well and could tell that I was not right. My senior year coach, Elisha Brewer, also saw the terrified look in my eyes. They both were headed in my direction. I literally froze and tears began to stream down my face. I was not quite sure what was happening but I was losing it. I imagined myself not doing well. I saw myself losing the race. I thought about not even going to the start line for the race. They both looked at me and of course were comforting but also reminded me quickly to snap out of it! They told me that I was here and I was here for a reason. I struggled to hear what they were saying, until it suddenly hit me. I had worked hard just like all my other competitors, and I needed to trust in myself and to believe in myself. It was TIME, it was time for me to put my fears aside and BELIEVE. Everyone else always believed in me and it was now time for Mary Danner to believe in herself. I could do this I told myself, I could really get myself together and put my best foot forward. I would make sure to leave nothing behind and put it all on the track. Experiencing this reminded me that it is always nice to be able to have close friends and coaches to speak life to you. By saying that, I mean to encourage me, allow me to see my potential and make the most of my opportunity. I was thankful for that intervention because I don't know what I would have done without those ladies. I realized that I needed to put on my big girl panties, and get to that line with fire in my heart. This was my moment and I wasn't going to let anything stop me.

That day I was able to race to a personal best in the 400 meters for the University of Cincinnati. I clocked 53.30 in the 400 meters, set the school record, placed 2nd in the Conference USA Meet and made trying to qualify for NCAAs a possibility. Also in the meet, I ran a great 200 meters, and a good 4x400 meter relay leg. I had never tried to look toward attending the NCAAs. In my head I wasn't good enough and I didn't think I could get there. After seeing my time at conference, I wanted to try and attend a last-chance meet to attempt to lower my time down even more. I came up short and ended my college career never winning a conference title and never qualifying for the NCAA Championships. That day I realized that we must never wait until the last minute to go for our goals. If I had built up my courage and entered the season saying I'm going to the NCAAs, my story may have been different. Perhaps I needed to go through that for a reason.

That year, 2002, Chris, the guy I had been dating made headlines for the University of Cincinnati. I did too. We were destined for greatness and maybe, as some would say, destined for a future together. There was an article printed on May 20, 2002 by Shawn Sell that stated, "Junior, Chris Wineberg (South Vienna, Ohio/Northeastern), and senior, Mary Danner (Cincinnati, Ohio/Walnut Hills), were named the most valuable performers on the University of Cincinnati track and field teams at the team's annual awards banquet. Wineberg had earned the men's award after winning the Conference USA decathlon and earning an NCAA provisional mark, he was also the All Ohio decathlon champion, and finished third at the prestigious Drake Relays. He was coached by Jim Schnur. The head coach of the men's team, Bill Schnier said, that "Chris has passion and skill in everything that he does."

The article also went on to state that Danner broke her own school record in the 400 meters at the Conference USA Championships (53.30) and earned five first place finishes that year. She also owned the second best time on the team in the 200 meters (24.68) while helping the 4x400 meter relay to a school record. The head coach for the women's team was Jim Schnur and he stated that Mary "was the best quarter miler and a dominant force on the 4x400 relay. The qualities of her races were excellent."

I was so proud after that meet! I was graduating from college with my degree, but I was unsure if I was really ready to hang up my spikes. I wanted to see if I could take running to the next level. I didn't think about the Olympics, but I knew I wanted to keep going. I had a newfound belief in my talent and in myself. Chris was an inspiration. I admired him throughout our college years and his ability to be a leader to his teammates. He was a motivator to all and a good teammate. He competed fearlessly and always had confidence. He encouraged me—made me feel that I could accomplish it all too.

Little did we both know the great things we would accomplish on the track together!

# SEVEN

## So You Want
## to be a Track Star

Track is such a beautiful sport that allows one to pursue their dreams and attain many goals. It is an amazing opportunity to be able to run with gazelle-like qualities, and push yourself to many different limits and levels. But, most of all, track allows you to be YOU.-Mary Wineberg 2013

I knew that I wanted to find a job and I wanted to pursue running post--collegiately. My mom was very proud of me for getting my college degree because, to her, education came first and all other things were secondary. She was a strong believer in God and always prayed that I would do something productive with my life. She was excited to attend my last meet of the season and really admired all of my accomplishments so far. She was a good mother, and I couldn't ask for anything more. I can honestly say that through those pivotal years, I had not thought about my birth mother. After being adopted, it was no longer something I dwelled on. No one had heard from her. I was now a college graduate, an adult who now had to face the real world on my own. I had been set up with the fundamentals and now it was time for me to put those skills to the test. Athens raised me well, to be independent, driven, respectful, and have the ability to speak up when needed. I was now going to continue to be the best that I could be. I looked into the mirror and I finally saw a beautiful young lady who could feel comfortable in her own skin, who wasn't embarrassed to be tall anymore. I was now able to walk in three-inch heels with my head held high and not have a worry about who was watching or even commenting about me. I was finally happy with being me.

I started to think more and more about my next steps. What did I want to do? Did I love track enough to pursue it after college? The clock was ticking and I would have to make some decisions. I had talked to my mom about possibly pursuing my professional career and still trying to run at the same time. She didn't understand why I would have the desire to run track after college. She had a lot of questions and I truly did not have all the answers. This was going to be something new for the both of us. Athens and I both decided that we would pray on it and see from there. I was excited about my new goal and no matter what I decided, there were still many people supporting me.

My sorority line sisters from college were amazing. They supported my dreams and in their eyes I was already a track star, even though I knew I had a long way to go. Chris, who I was still dating, was also a great support. He still had two more years of college. He was majoring in mechanical engineering which was a five-year program and I was one year ahead of him in school. I looked into some different opportunities and came across a semi-professional team that was sponsored by Nike and headed up by a man who was committed to the sport. He wanted to help athletes reach their potential and go beyond their college careers. I had a couple of friends running for this team and a former college teammate. I was excited to be added to their roster. I would now be moving to Indianapolis, Indiana and becoming an Indiana Invader.

I took a job as a health promotions manager for Cardiac Rehab in a senior group home facility. I would work from 7:00 a.m. to 3:00

p.m. and then train immediately after my workday was over. My life there was limited and I often missed home. I had many more friends in Cincinnati so I would drive back home every weekend just to see my family and friends. It was very different training by myself or training in a small group rather than a large team like I had done at UC. I didn't officially have a coach, but I was able to get some help and pointers from a coach who was helping my former UC teammate, Brandon Hon. Coach Clinton Davis would write up workouts for us and we would then have to be committed to executing them on our own. It was a struggle, but I had learned to be quite independent. I missed my mom, my family, my sands, my friends and I missed Chris. I missed my life in Cincinnati.

I was so grateful for this wonderful opportunity to be in Indianapolis pursuing a dream of running post-collegiately, and it was through this experience that I got to meet a lot of other individuals with the same goals in mind. These individuals were some of the people who, to this day I appreciate for helping me become more invested in the sport. I was able to learn about the history and what is expected of an athlete training at this level. I qualified for my first USA Track and Field Championship in 2003 during the indoor season. I was excited, pumped, but also nervous. The meet was in Boston, and I remember gearing myself up for the open 400. I surprised a lot of people when I made the final. At that time, I did not know how significant it was to make the final! I was just excited to be there at the meet. Making the final meant that I was eligible to run on the USA 4x400 relay team at the US Indoor World Championships. I couldn't believe that I had secured my spot and made my first indoor international team! I was so proud to call my mom to tell her the good news. This good news meant being able to wear Team USA on my chest. It meant getting lots of uniform pieces and a suitcase full of gear. I thought, "Wow, I made it." I vowed to myself that, "This is step one for all of the many additional steps that I will take to make a name for myself on the running circuit. I'm willing to put in the work that will get me there and beyond."

The indoor world championship meet was held in Birmingham, England and I can remember getting on the flight and being so excited. I would be running for Team USA. I went to the meet with an open mind and high hopes. I arrived at the hotel and made plans to go see the indoor track stadium. Here my eyes just lit up. I was amazed at all of the track athletes with whom I had made the team, such as Gail Devers, Tyree Washington, Jerome Young, Justin Gatlin, Derek Miles, Jenny Adams, and Christie Gaines... just to name a few. These individuals had made a name for themselves in the sport. It was amazing to realize that this young girl from Cincinnati, Ohio was on the team with these individuals, and I wanted to make a name for myself as well. Since I was not a standout in college, so many people did not know who I was or where I came from. It gave me great pleasure to say, "Yes, I am from the University of Cincinnati." Of course, we were known for our basketball program mostly and I got many comments about the men's basketball program and Bob Huggins. People were amazed because they had never actually heard about the track program. Most of the athletes that had made the team were from major track programs like LSU, South Carolina, Texas A&M and Florida.

I knew that I would be assigned a roommate but I didn't know who it would be. I only knew one other person who had made the team and I was hoping we would be roommates. I had met Tiffany, also a 400m runner, at the indoor USA Championships. I thought she was an amazing athlete and when we saw each other, we were like "Wow, we made it, we're here!" I was impressed that I would not have to come out of pocket for anything for this trip. Everything was paid for. The flight, the gear, the shoes, the meals and the hotel room ... it was like living on top of the world. I was amazed at the hospitality of USA Track and Field. I headed to my roomslowly pulling my suitcase. I found my room, unlocked the door and put everything down. I immediately laid on the bed ... and I had my little "Wow" moment where I said, "If this is what it means to run track professionally, I think I want to do this all the time."

There was a knock on the door and my roommate walked in. Well, I assumed it was my roommate. She had her bags and had unlocked the door with a key. As she walked in, I immediately sat up and said, "Hey, my name is Mary Danner. What's your name?"

She quietly said hello and responded back with, "My name is Allyson, nice to meet you."

At this moment I wasn't quite sure who she was and what event she ran, but she looked really young. I did remember watching some of the events from the USA indoor Nationals but not much. I was so consumed with my event, and it being my first time ever there. I probably missed out on a lot of other events and realizing what other athletes who had also made the team. We immediately started to chat and me, being the talker I am, probably almost scared the poor girl away. No, just kidding, but I did ask her questions and we got to know each other a little bit. This young girl was so polite and humble and she didn't seem to be bothered at all by my talkative self. I learned that she was there to run the 200m. I had not gotten a chance to call my mom and let her know that I had made it, so I called to tell her all about my travels and to make sure she was doing ok.

A couple days later I finally called and talked to Chris and since I was in England I had to use a calling card to place the call. Man, these calling cards were the best thing ever. I did not have a cell phone, but they worked like magic. Prior to flying to the meet the suggestion was that we get calling cards to be able to communicate with our family back home. Chris was excited to hear all about my travels and how things were progressing. We talked about the food, the track, my practices and we talked about my roommate. I told him that I was happy to have what seemed to be an easy roommate, one who wasn't annoying and one who didn't snore. He listened to me tell all about her, how she seemed to be an awesome girl. She was so sweet, kind, polite, had very good manners, and was humble. The only weird thing was that she was only a 16-year-old highschooler. He immediately asked if my roommate's name was Allyson Felix. "Mary, do you know who she is? She is an absolute phenome and was on the cover of Track and Field News!"

I was surprised to find out that the girl that I would be rooming with for the next four days or so was actually one of the best high school athletes in the world. Little did I know that she would go on to become one of the greatest track and field athletes in the history of the world and that five years later we would make history together, winning Olympic Gold on the 4x400 relay. She was a wonderful roommate and I am honored that I met her then. It's ironic that we both made our first USA team together. We were six years apart in age. I had been out of college for a year and she still had a year of high school left. Little did Allyson know, but meeting her in 2003 gave me a lot of hope in myself that I could achieve anything. Just the mere fact that she was sixteen years old and made the team allowed me to want to set goals and push myself even higher. She would be an inspiration to me for the years to come. Thank you, Allyson, for that!

I also got the opportunity to meet and become very good friends with two male 400 meter runners. At that time, they were like my big brothers. They looked out for me and gave me great advice. They wanted me to have a good experience as a newcomer to this level of track and field. They said, "We're here to help you, to give you guidance, and to encourage you to become the best 400 meter runner that you can be."

I was very thankful to hear those words that came from them. I pretended that I had figured out this track and field world and I didn't want to seem too naive. I wanted to jump up and down screaming in excitement that I was getting pointers from two established professionals, but, of course, I had to maintain my cool. There was something different about those two. They were very genuine and respected me, even as a new athlete to the sport. They ended up giving me encouragement each time that I ran on the track, not only from that year of 2003, but through the next couple of years as well. It was just amazing to interact with such humble and great people. I thank them for everything because they gave me an opportunity to ask a lot of questions and start to understand this foreign track world. They explained that everyone would try to give me advice now and they really helped me filter out whom I should and should not listen to. They both assured me that if I kept working hard, I was going to do some amazing things.

Finally, it was competition time at the 2003 Indoor World Championships. I will admit I was very nervous. I remember watching my teammates gearing up and getting ready to compete in the 400. I watched their every move, how they warmed up, when they drank water and how they carried themselves. I had the 4x4 coming up and I had to tell myself that wow, this isn't the college team anymore, this is the big leagues, this is Team USA. The athletes here meant business and it wasn't a game to them. Leading up to the 4x400 race I had plenty of jitters and nerves, but I vowed to myself that I was never again going to have a breakdown as in my senior year in college. The thoughts tried to surface, but I told myself that I was too strong for this now. My mind would not get the best of me. I was actually scheduled to be an alternate for the 4x400 relay based on my place at indoor nationals. The USA team traveled two alternates for the relay and I was the 2nd alternate. When it was actually time for the coaches to make the final decision on who would run, I was surprised they picked me. They said, "You have fresh legs, you have drive and determination, and we believe in you."

Once I found out that I would be running, I knew it was game time. My teammates for the 4x4 consisted of Monique Hennagan, Megan Addy, and Brenda Taylor. Monique Hennagan was a star in my eyes. She had qualified for World's in the open 400 meters and had already made an Olympic team. She was an inspiration and motivated me to want to become a better 400 meter runner. Just seeing her tenacity and personality on and off the track was inspiring. It allowed me to see that these athletes are real people, only with more accolades on their resumes.

During my leg of the race, I had never encountered the hostility that I experienced running the 4x4 at this level. I remember being jolted and being knocked aside by a 400 meter runner from Jamaica and not knowing what to do. I was so shocked when she bumped me, and I said in my mind, "Oh no, this isn't fair! She's not allowed to do that!"

I had to realize that, yeah, in this 4x4 it can get dirty, and it can sometimes get ugly. But it's about how strong-willed you are. I almost fell off of my rhythm pattern as I was running, and I was thinking in my mind, "My team's gonna be disappointed in me because I wasn't able to give my best after being bumped into and almost tripping off the track." I still fought through, and we ended up finishing third, getting a bronze medal that year in 2003 in Birmingham. It was exciting to be able to get on the podium and receive an award. This was my first medal ever for Team USA.

I still have my competition uniform from that meet, and I cherish the medal I received. Many people were shocked to see me on the podium. They questioned: who is Mary Danner, where did she come from? They had never seen me at the NCAAs, and wondered how I had qualified in such a top level meet. The meet came to a close, but I made sure to get email addresses and contact information from some key people. The relay coach for that indoor team was Orin Richburg and I met a coach by the name of Brooks Johnson who also saw something in me. He and Orin were putting together a high-performance relay team, where athletes would run different meets all over in the outdoor season. It would be called the High Performance Relay Project. They wanted me to take part! Not only did I come home with a medal, but I came home with some information that I now had to digest. I accepted the invitation to be a part of the High Performance Relay Project and once again impressed the coaches at the Penn Relays. I battled the same girl that bumped me at the Indoor World Championships, but this time I avoided her contact, moved ahead of her, and ran my fastest time ever. After that race, Brooks Johnson invited me to train at the Olympic Training Center in Chula Vista, California to prepare for the 2004 Olympic Trials. "Wow, someone wants me to move across the country and train with them! What should I do?"

I had been training, as I stated before, in Indianapolis with no coach. I didn't really know what I wanted to do, but I knew that I wanted to try out for the Olympics in 2004. They were coming up in a year, and it would be a new goal--to train and make the team for Athens 2004.

After meeting with them and hearing all that they had to say, I was very interested. These guys sounded like they knew what they were talking about, and I wanted to experience something different, something new to get me to where I needed to be. I remember my two 400-meter male teammates telling me to always listen, ask a lot of questions and determine if it is in my best interest to keep listening. I felt good about our conversation and I felt like I could trust them. One talked fast, but with good information, and the other was smooth, calm and collected. They were both established coaches. I had heard good things about them, and I was delighted that they wanted to work with me. I came home and talked to my mom: "You know what? I think I have a wonderful opportunity that's being presented to me. I would love to make it work."

I had gone from living about an hour and a half away from home. Now I would possibly be moving all the way to California to train for the 2004 Olympic Games. Never in my life did I ever imagine moving that far away from my mom. I struggled with this decision quite a bit, because I know that living in Indianapolis was a little harder for me. I couldn't make those quick drives over to my mom's house if her sugar got low. I really was just too far away. I had to depend on my family in Cincinnati, and I really had to depend on Chris. Chris was such a blessing to my family. What other guy would say to you, especially if you're not even married, "You know what, Mary? I know that you're trying to pursue your dreams. I'll check on your mom while you're away. If you can't get in touch with her, I'll drive over and make sure that everything is okay." Chris was also excited to tell me that this opportunity sounded legit and I shouldn't let it pass me by. We came up with a plan and decided we would still date each other, and we were going to try to make it work.

I was so thankful to hear that Chris would check on my mom and we would still stay together. It's difficult to be a caregiver to someone who is older; you tend to be very protective of them. My mom, who struggled with managing her diabetes, seemed to be a delicate case. I loved her with all of my heart, but I didn't want to put my dreams on hold. She wanted me to make the most of my opportunities as well. I contacted Coach Brooks and told him I was coming. I didn't know what exactly it would entail and I didn't know how hard these workouts were going to be. I didn't even know if I was going to mesh with this coach, and I didn't know who my training partners would be at the training center, but sometimes you have to take the risk. I was ready for the risk.

I was being offered the opportunity to train at the Olympic Training Center in Chula Vista, California for a year. I had never been there. The only thing I knew about it was what Chris had told me about it. The year before, he went on a family vacation to California and they stopped in at the Olympic Training Center for a few hours. Chris could only tell me that it was a neat place and pretty amazing. I did end up doing my own research on it. It was interesting to see all the opportunities and who could go there as a resident to use their facilities. You had to either be invited, or you had to have been running times that would make you eligible to attend. Knowing that I would be coached by such an exceptional coach got me excited. I did some research about Coach Brooks Johnson. I found out that he had some great accolades; he was a former sprinter who ran on the 4x1 in 1963 and attained a gold medal at the Pan American Games. Not only did he coach some great athletes in the past, but he coached at Stanford. He had also coached some Olympians. I remember when I first met him. He had on a straw hat and cowboy boots, but I kept thinking 'this man means business.' What type of training would I encounter? I was very nervous.

I packed my things, said my goodbyes, and headed to the airport. I felt at peace knowing Athens would be okay. I remember her reassurance. She said, "Don't worry about me. Go out there, learn a lot, and do your best." I gave my mom and Chris each a big hug and kiss and headed to board my plane. When I landed in California, looked out my window, and could only see mountains, and it suddenly hit me. This was nothing like Cincinnati and I immediately started to miss home. I got off the plane and realized that I had to try to make this my new home away from home. As the taxi drove into the gates of the facility, I can remember seeing the Olympic Rings and getting goose bumps: "Wow. I am at the United States Olympic Training Center."

Once I was settled in, I had the opportunity to meet some people who were already staying there, and some other athletes who would be in my training group. The training group consisted of about ten of us. There were two other female 400-meter runners, but I did not know them very well. I had raced against one in college and had met the other one at the Indoor USA Nationals. These two girls, Tia and Tiffany, ended up being great training partners. We were all part of the High Performance Relay Project. Training in California was a great experience. We had two-a-day practices, were able to run on the beach, and I was pushed to my limits in the workouts. I remember keeping a training log and learning how to write down the things that I would do for training, how I ran the workouts, how my body felt and what I would eat.

Everything was great, but I missed home. I hated being in a different time zone than Cincinnati. The three-hour time difference made it tough to talk with everyone back home. There were many days that I just wanted to cry because I was missing home so much. I flew home once every three months because I wanted to see my friends, family, and Chris. I wanted to also be able to tell everyone what I was doing in California. I learned so much that year. I learned how to eat properly and the importance of nutrition for an elite athlete. Everyone met with a sports psychologist and I learned how to not let my mind hold me back. I learned how to lift correctly and I became a stronger athlete. I learned how to utilize treatments such as a massage and chiropractic care to ensure that my body was recovering and able to be at its best. This facility had everything and there was no need for me to leave the center and go off site. The housing arrangements were like college dorms and the cafeteria provided all of our meals and snacks. I didn't have to cook or figure out my own meals. I didn't have to buy my recovery shakes or Gatorades. Everything was taken care of for us. With all of this help, would I be in a position to make the 2004 Olympic Team? I enjoyed my new training partners and it reminded me a lot of college, just much more difficult and we were much more focused at practice.

Midway through the year, I was reunited with one of my teammates I had looked up to at the Indoor World Championship. He came to train with us at the center and it felt great to have him join the group. He was a great resource to answer my questions about running professionally and he was a great training partner. It felt good to be back with my "big brother," and Tyre was such a humble guy. We were both 400 meter runners, and we were both trying to attain the same goal. I realized that I could learn a lot from him. To this day, he still serves as a mentor to me. It's amazing what networking can do for you in the sport of track and field. There were times and there were days when I didn't understand why the workouts were so hard.

Why did this coach want me to run 800s? Why was he pushing me to these limits? He was pushing us to strengthen us physically, but also to make us mentally stronger. He was always instilling his wisdom onto us. He told me, "As you're training, preparing and getting ready for big competition meets, you don't change anything when you get to those big meets. You keep doing what got you there. **What got you here will keep you here.**" He also would say, "Your biggest thing that can mess you up is what is between your ears, which is your brain. Your mind can mess you up. You have to learn how to be mentally strong."

My training was going well. I was running some excellent times in practice. I was able to adjust to Coach Brook's training and I think he was pleased. I was getting better and better. My times were starting to drop and I was gearing up to be ready for the Olympic trials. The 2004 Olympic trials were going to be held in Sacramento, California. During this year of training, I had so many great stories and experiences to share with my mom, Chris and my friends. The opportunity of being at the training center was truly a blessing.

It was finally time and we headed to the 2004 Olympic trials. Coach Brooks reminded all of us that we were ready! He told me that I just have to get out there and I have to run. He reminded me that I had been dropping my times in the 400 and that I even ran a couple of good 800 meter times. I was pretty pumped and I was ready to go. You could not have told me that year in 2004, that I would not make the Olympic team. Everything was happening for me, from making an indoor team, to winning a medal and being able to travel to so many different meets as part of the high-performance relay team. Now I was able to train at the Olympic Center with so many resources. I had a lot of support at the meet in 2004. Both Athens and Chris came to the meet. Two of my sorority sisters, Natalie and Kertrice, traveled and made posters to support me. Also my god-sister, Adriane, and her husband, Rod, came to cheer me on. I was now at my first ever Olympic trials. What would I do? How would it turn out? Would I believe in myself to get through the meet? This meet had even more great athletes there than at the Indoor World Championships. I was star struck by Justin Gatlin, Stacy Dragila, Gail Devers, Joanna Hayes, Jamie Nieto, Marion Jones, Hazel Clark, and Jearl Miles Clark to name a few. I was in awe of these athletes and wanted to be on their level and be like them.

I ran well in the preliminary round and advanced to the semifinal. Stepping onto the line of the women's 400 semi-final was a day that I remember so well. It was my first day since college in which I felt as if I was the underdog. I was very nervous. I was shaking. I was thinking 'I can't do this.' This was beyond anything that I had ever done or tried to accomplish. I had so many people in the stands supporting me and I didn't want to let them down. The gun went off. I remember taking off and it seemed as if I was running in slow motion. I could see everything occurring around me like it was a dream. All the big names in the women's 400 had gotten around the first curve before me. They got to the backstretch before me, they entered the final curve before me, and coming home the last 100m I was still in the back. I felt as if I had this out-of-body experience and was telling myself, 'Mary, run faster. You can do this. Run faster,' but my legs would not turn over. My arms were trying to pump, but I wasn't going anywhere fast. I crossed the line in dead last and was in such disbelief. I had run 52.85 and had gotten beat by DeeDee Trotter, Monique Henderson, Monique Hennagan, Sanya Richards, to name a few. The day before I had run 51.88 and I was thinking that the next round would be a piece of cake. I clearly was not prepared to run all the rounds at the trials. I was a fresh new kid to this sport and that was something that I would have to learn how to master. My Olympic dream was over. I did not make the final of the women's 400 and I was truly devastated. What hurt worse was the fact that everything had been going so well for me. I had moved to California and put everything into this dream and now what did I have to show for it? What was I going to do now? I left the meet in tears, and I questioned whether or not I wanted to continue to run track. I figured that these girls were way out of my league and I could never compete with them. They were fast and strong and had so many accolades already.

After the race, I talked with my coach about what may have gone wrong. I didn't know why I had done so badly. Things were looking so good for me prior to the meet, and then everything went to shambles. I thought of it as failure when I didn't make the Olympic Team. I thought, "Wow, see? This is exactly what I was afraid of. I was afraid to fail, and I did just that."

I failed. I failed completely. I failed and I had let my friends and my family down, and those who were there to support me. I honestly didn't know what to say to them when they asked me, "Well, what happened? How did the race feel for you?"

All I could say to them was, "It just wasn't my time, I guess." Or, "It wasn't meant to be." Or, "Honestly, I don't know what happened."

I had my moments of crying it out. I had my moments of questioning "Why?" After the trials, I packed up my things and headed back to Cincinnati to try to figure out what to do with my life. On the plane ride home I had many hours to think, and it finally hit me. I did have something to show for my time spent at the training center. I had come in as an inexperienced athlete who was interested in bettering her training and had left with some growth, some improvements and mostly a brand new attitude. I didn't want to feel sorry for myself; instead, I wanted to prove others wrong. I wanted to show that I could make it in the track and field world. I knew that the Lord still had a plan for me and was still by my side. I needed to continue to be strong and not give up.

Joshua 1:9

"Be strong and courageous; do not be frightened or dismayed,
for the Lord your God is with you wherever you go."

I was truly happy to be back with my family and friends in
Cincinnati, but I would have to settle for watching the Olympics on
TV that year. It just wasn't my time to make the Olympic team. I knew
that I would have to be more faithful with my gift, more disciplined
and more determined. After getting over the disappointment, I was so
happy and eager to make the next season even bigger and better. This
learning opportunity set me up to know what it takes to train for the
Olympics. Athens had supported my dream of moving to California
and now after the Olympic trials I was back home. She reminded me
that I needed to get a life. In this regard, she meant for me to figure
out what I was going to do with myself now. She didn't fully understand the whole training thing and that this was a true commitment.
This meant giving your all and making sacrifices and realizing that if
it didn't work, you could try again. I explained to her that I wanted to
continue running track and training for the next Olympics. She didn't
know that the track circuit consisted of many meets all over the world
and it was not just about training for the Olympics. It would be training for each year and each event that I could be invited to.

Chris and I were happy to be able to see each other daily; having a
long distance relationship was very hard. We had so much to catch up
on. While I was in California, Chris had accomplished a lot. He gradu-
ated with his degree in Mechanical Engineering. He also went to the
NCAAs, placed 8th in the decathlon and reached his goal of becoming an All-American. He was being coached by Jim Schnur, who was
also my college coach. Coach Jim himself had once been an amazing
high level track athlete. In college he qualified for the NCAAs in both
the 400 meters and the decathlon. Post-collegiately he competed for

TEAM USA in a few international meets. His highest ranking was 4th in the U.S. in the decathlon. He had been known as a standout 220 yard and 440 yard sprinter in high school and had won the state title. Now that I was back I needed a coach, especially if I was still going to train. I was still part of the High Performance Relay pool and would have opportunities to run in meets such as the Penn Relays, the Texas relays, and the TSU Relays. I would be able to wear Team USA on my chest at these events. The continuation of the Relay Project allowed me to be exposed to more high level track and field. I needed a coach. I asked Jim if he would coach me, and I was so excited that he agreed. Jim Schnur was definitely the right man and coach for the job. He was an awesome choice to help advance my career to the next level and not only had he already worked with me in college, but he was quite aware of my potential. He knew me, he knew my training abilities, and he knew many things that we needed to fix to get me on the right path to success. I was now a different athlete than what I had been in the past. I wasn't the immature athlete from college who was still learning the ropes. I instead was a woman who had many goals in mind. I wanted to be the best and I wanted to be serious about my training. I also wanted to get serious about life and my future.

Chris and I talked about marriage during this time. We both were on the same page in that we wanted to be with each other and were willing to see where the future would take us. My mom really liked Chris. Chris had also talked with her regarding a possible engagement in the future and she was very supportive. She was happy that I was growing up, but I needed to find a way to support myself. I wanted to be a teacher. It was one of my passions. I found a job in education and committed myself to training after work each day. I trained with Coach Jim and he wanted to fix my running technique. He wanted me to get stronger and he wanted me to train like my competitors. During that year of training and competing, things did not go as hoped. I battled with some injuries, but still made it to nationals.

At the 2005 USA nationals, I once again went home disappointed after I was not able to make it to the final. I was starting to get even more frustrated and doubted once again if track was the right choice for me. Then to make matters even worse, unbelievable news broke regarding drug use in track and field. Did I even want to be associated with this sport anymore?

I remember turning on the TV and being in shock at what was occurring. The BALCO scandal was heating up and I literally sat in front of the TV in total disbelief. I immediately called Chris from the next room to come watch. My eyes were glued to the as an American athlete that I had known admitted to using performance enhancing drugs. I could not believe it! Some of these athletes being named, I had looked up to for years, and they were on DRUGS. Yes, that is right—the five letter word that no one wants to ever say. I was in shock; at the fact that I had no idea that drug use was going on within the sport. I suppose that I was slightly naive. I wanted to believe that when an athlete ran or did something amazing, it came from their God-given talent and work ethic. Boy was I wrong in some cases.

One of the most decorated athletes of all time, one who I looked up to and even had a book signed by her was in the middle of the scandal. I was devastated to find out that she was one of the many track and field athletes being named. From that moment on I was educated about what some athletes were doing in my sport and it was sad. They had gotten away with it for years, but were now being caught. Someone had sent in a syringe full of the performance enhancing drug to the testing federation to alert them of what was going on in the sport. This was big news and I knew that I never wanted to be involved in anything like this. I am happy to say that I was never approached by anyone regarding taking drugs to improve my performance on the track. I was blessed to be surrounded by so many positive and honest people who would never allow that to occur. I told my coach about this scandal and I was surprised that he wasn't shocked. When he was competing in the '80s, he had heard of drug use by athletes. I reminded my coach that he would never, ever have to worry about me and DRUGS. I tried to stay positive even though what was occurring was tarnishing the sport. I didn't dwell on pointing fingers or trying to figure out if the girls lining up with me in the 400 were or weren't on drugs. I committed that I would do it the right way and still make it to the top.

These athletes that chose to use drugs would eventually pay for their wrongdoing. Medals were stripped and performances were annulled. This scandal was the scandal of the year. It created a lot of buzz at the track meets, within the media, and had all the athletes aware and talking. It was sad. I'm sure not everyone involved was a bad person, as portrayed by the media, but they certainly made some very bad choices. It goes to show that even good people can make horrible mistakes. I'm sure they wish they could take it back and not let it ruin their careers. I vowed to never be involved or be taken into this realm of the sport. I was going to compete honestly and with the utmost dignity.

# EIGHT

## A New Plan

Although my 2005 track season ended in disappointment, it was a very exciting year in my life. Chris proposed to me and I was thrilled to say yes! My life was headed in the right direction. I was excited to plan my wedding and I was excited to prepare for the upcoming track season. 2006 was going well, but we weren't really getting anywhere. I wasn't getting into the big meets where I could actually make a living running track and Chris was experiencing some of the same problems. This was his 2nd year training post-collegiately and with the challenges of working to support himself, he wasn't able to put in the time required to make improvements in the decathlon over his college performances. We would both be out there on the track, grinding away after work, but it wasn't enough and it wasn't working.

Something had to change. Something had to change dramatically if we wanted to achieve a different result. This was my 4th year running track post-collegiately and I hadn't achieved the level of success I was looking for. I was putting more money into training and travel for meets than I was earning. I was discouraged about running. Was it really worth all the time and sacrifice? Was this what God wanted me to do and pursue. I loved being a teacher, but training after work each day just wasn't working. My competitors did not have to endure all this; well, at least not the ones who were top ten in the world. They had contracts and were paid by their shoe sponsors. They were also making an income from running at various meets all over the world and would even get bonuses when they ran well. I wanted that! I had a great coach who had a plethora of knowledge in the 400. I wanted to have a good agent who was willing to work hard for me. I was ready for a change. I knew God had more in store for me, but why wasn't I seeing it yet? Chris was trying to balance developing a real estate business, working a part-time engineering job, working as a part-time track coach at UC, and then training for the decathlon after all that. It wasn't working. He was struggling in his training and starting to put more energy into his role as a part-time track coach at UC. We were two broke wannabe track stars scheduled to be married in just a few months. I came up with a plan, a bold plan, but how would Chris respond?

One evening, in May of 2006, I laid out the plan for him. "I want to quit my job and run track full-time. I think I can make the European circuit this summer, but I need you to be my training partner."

At first he didn't know how to respond. He wanted to help me, but this would mean officially giving up on his own Olympic dreams. Was I selfish to even ask this of him? Would this damage our relationship or is this what couples do for each other when they love each other and are together? He had to think things over and take an honest look at how he was doing as an athlete. He knew he was going to come up short that season of qualifying for nationals, so he made the switch and started training with me each day. He ran every workout with me and always stayed just one step ahead. I could tell it was not an easy transition for him, but we started to find our groove. I quit my job and made sure I was doing everything right. I was sleeping at least eight hours each night. I was eating right and doing the little things that I hadn't had the time for when I was working. I spent time in the training room before and after each practice taking care of my body and making sure I felt good.

We started really enjoying the time spent training together and my times started to drop as well. He commented how it was getting tougher and tougher to stay ahead of me in the workouts. I headed into the 2006 USA Nationals with a new found confidence.

At nationals, I easily advanced through the preliminary round. I made it through the semi-final round and finally made it to my first final at USA outdoors. In the final, I ran a new PR of 51.27 finishing 5th overall and made my first outdoor team as a relay alternate. This was not a World Championship year or an Olympic year, but I was able to represent Team USA in the World Cup. The plan seemed to be working. The month of training with Chris and completely dedicating myself to the sport helped me to run a new PR. What if I followed this plan for the entire 2007 season?

# NINE

## Breakthrough

I remember that special day in which Chris asked me to be his wife. It was one of the best days of my life! I would soon be Mrs. Wineberg. I had been running as Mary Danner and I was excited to start running as Mary Wineberg. Would I confuse people, and how would it sound when the announcers of the meets would say my name? I guess we would eventually find out.

Chris and I were married on August 5th, 2006 and the day went off without a hitch. We had planned well and made the most of the moment. My wedding colors were pink and silver. I figured a girl could never love too much pink, and since I was an AKA it was a perfect color choice. Silver was picked to accent the pink, but if you would have let me pick the color for the guys, I would have selected green. Chris was not going to let that happen and we agreed on silver. The tables for the reception were all done with an Olympic theme in mind. Each table was named after a city from a previous Olympic Games. The Olympic dream was in my heart and was even displayed in my wedding. Everyone who attended and took part in our wedding day fully enjoyed themselves. It was my fairytale wedding and we were starting a new life together. After our wonderful day and union, we traveled to the Dominican Republic for our honeymoon.

I wanted to enjoy my honeymoon to the fullest, but I also had to keep in mind that I had been selected to serve as an alternate for the women's 4x400 meter relay for the 2006 Outdoor World Cup team in Athens, Greece. Once I got back from my honeymoon, I was headed off on another plane to get to the meet. The life of an athlete: always on the go, traveling, the commitments, dedication and sacrifices that must be made. I ended up not running in the meet because they didn't need me, but I fulfilled my duties as an alternate, warming up with the team just in case. It was still an awesome experience to be part of TEAM USA once again.

I was more excited and focused than ever for the 2007 season. I was so happy to have married a man who didn't mind this lifestyle. Not only did he support me in deciding to quit my job, but he even became my training partner and was excited to continue in that role. The 2007 season was going great. My times were dropping and I had more confidence than ever in my running abilities leading into USA Nationals. They were to be held right in Indianapolis, Indiana. This venue was so close to me that I could just drive there rather than fly to California or Iowa like I had done in the past. The meet was on the same track that I used to train on when I ran for the Indiana Invaders. I saw this as an advantage for me.

The meet was going well and I breezed through the prelims as well as the semifinals. I ran 51.15 in the prelims and then 51.06 in the semi-final. To make the 2007 Outdoor World Team, I would need to finish in the top 3 to qualify in the open 400 meters and top 6 for the relay.

I was in the final, but now look at what I was up against. I was filled with emotion: nervousness, fear, even questioning if I could run the race. The other 7 lanes were filled with women who on paper had way more talent than me. All of their resumes and accolades put me to shame. The other lanes were filled with women that were World-ranked or had won Olympic Medals, set national records, won NCAA titles, or won multiple state titles in high school. Everyone in the race had accomplished some of these things, that is, except for me.

Then came the lane assignments. The announcer highlighted each athlete's accomplishments and I grew even more nervous. This is how he introduced each runner:

Lane 1: Shana Cox- three time high school national champion, NCAA runner up, and still in college at Penn State.

Lane 2: Mousha Robinson- two time state champion, eleven time NCAA All-American while at Texas, and an Olympic Gold Medalist.

Lane 3: Monique Henderson – World Junior champion in 2002, Set the high school national record at 50.74, ran at UCLA and is an Olympic Gold Medalist.

Lane 4: Sanya Richards – American record holder and ranked #1 in the World in the 400m and is an Olympic Gold Medalist.

Lane 5: DeeDee Trotter – State Champion in Georgia, NCAA champion while at Tennessee, placed in the Olympic final while still in college. And an Olympic Gold Medalist.

Lane 6: Mary Wineberg - 57.8 in high school, never made the state meet final in Ohio, never won conference title in college while at the University of Cincinnati, never qualified for the NCAA's while in college, no Olympic experience.

Lane 7: Natasha Hastings – World youth champion and World Junior champion. NCAA champion and still in college at South Carolina.

Lane 8: Monique Hennagan – Won the state meet in North Carolina in the 100, 200, and 400 three straight years and won USA junior nationals two straight years. Also, an Olympic Gold medalist.

All of these emotions were running through me. I had so many doubts that continued to try to creep into my mind, but I decided to put it all on the line. I wasn't going to defeat myself. I had worked hard and prepared for this moment. That decision, that race, that moment changed everything for me forever. The gun went off and I blasted out of the blocks, I continued to move well down the backstretch positioning myself where I needed to be in the race. With 150m to go, it was the moment of truth. I dug deep, believed in myself and tore down the homestretch moving from 6$^{th}$, to 5$^{th}$, to 4$^{th}$, and I finally moved into 3$^{rd}$ place just before crossing the finish line. Wow, my life flashed before me and I could not believe it. I had just passed the number one ranked athlete in the world, to claim the last USA spot for the open 400 meters at the World Championships. I had run a new personal record of 50.24 seconds. As I crossed the line, I immediately looked up at the scoreboard to make sure it was real. I clapped my hands in joy and thanked God for this blessing. I went over and congratulated all of the competitors in the race. I saw the look on Sanya's face. It was a face that I knew all too well, disappointment. I gave her a huge hug and told her that it would be okay and she would make it back on top. She was the best of the best and I knew that this moment was hard for her. I hugged Deedee and Natasha as well. They both were amazing ladies I had gotten to know through the years. I was excited to be representing TEAM USA both in the 400 meters and in the 4x400 relay at the World Championships.

Here are the final results from the race.

| | | |
|---|---|---|
| DeeDee Trotter | Adidas | 49.64 |
| Natasha Hastings | South Carolina | 49.84 |
| Mary Wineberg | Nike | 50.24 |
| Sanya Richards | Nike | 50.68 |
| Monique Henderson | Reebok | 50.82 |
| Monique Hennagan | Nike | 51.28 |
| Moushami Robinson | Nike | 51.47 |
| Shan Cox | Penn State | 52.23 |

I finally caught up to my family, my coach, and my agent, Andy Stubbs. They were so excited for me and everyone was really on cloud nine. My agent said that based on this performance everything was going to change for the better. He could get me into the "A" level races that had serious prize money and negotiate an improved contract with my shoe sponsor. My mom was starting to gain more of a perspective of the sport and she definitely understood that I had just done something big for myself and for my career. I was surprised by the time that I ran and it gave me a yearning to want to break that 50 second barrier in the women's 400. Making the team meant media interviews, team sign up, people who had never talked to me before saying congrats, meet directors saying that they wanted me in their meets and Nike was proud that I had made the team. I was on top of the world. I celebrated that night with my family and I knew the next day we would be back to the drawing board and back on the track in Cincinnati to train. Making that decision to quit my job was probably the right thing to do because now I would be traveling to more meets, making a living from running and being able to also get bonuses for times that I would run. I now had people saying, "Wow, did you see that Mary Wineberg? Where did she come from? Who is she?"

Coach Jim always had faith in me and believed that I could run like this. Now, I had to keep training like I wanted it. I had to keep training like I wanted to be the best in the world. I ran in several high profile European meets and on the day of our 1st wedding anniversary, August 5th, 2006, we boarded a plane for Osaka, Japan for the Track and Field World Championships. At the World Championships, in the open 400 I was the last American to run. No other American qualified automatically for the final. As my heat lined up, announcer Carol Lewis stated that Mary Wineberg has the Americans' hope on her shoulders. In the previous heat DeeDee Trotter had run and was waiting to see if she got in as a time qualifier. I crossed the line after my heat had gone and DeeDee sat on the sideline patiently looking at the clock. She had made it to the final too. I was so happy for the both of us; she had been such a good friend and role model to me through my years of running. To have made the final with her was an awesome experience. I sometimes jokingly called her my twin and she was really a pleasure just to be around, so joyful, funny and quite a character. She allowed me to continue to see the sport in a positive way. I admired that she started her campaign against drug use, called Test Me, I'm Clean.

Here at this meet, the U.S. would have two women in the 400 meter World final.

I ended up placing 8th in the world in the women's 400 meters and winning gold in the 4x400 relay. My teammates were all amazing and such great role models. I had formed everlasting friendships and all these ladies held a special place in my heart. I became close with some of them and I found that I could always call if I ever needed advice, or just wanted to say hello. I truly valued my teammates. The remainder of my season that year was spectacular. I was able to make a very nice income from running. I went to all the major meets and ran well into September when I finally came home from a long running circuit. I ended the season ranked 8th in the world in the 400 meters. It's amazing what time, faith, belief in yourself and perseverance can do. It's amazing what GOD can do and bestow in your life. Thank you to DeeDee, Monique Hennagan, Natasha, Sanya, and Allyson for being my teammates and gold medal winners that year in 2007. Without you all, none of this would have been possible.

# TEN

## An Olympic Dream

The year was now 2008 and I was coming off of the ultimate high of competing at the Outdoor World Championships. I still had Jim Schnur as my coach and my husband as my training partner. I was comfortable living in Cincinnati and appreciated being able to train at my alma mater, the University of Cincinnati. After my success in the previous season there was not a doubt in my mind that I could make the Olympic team. My coach and I sat down at the beginning of the year and planned out my season. He started off by asking me what some of my goals were and the things that I wanted to accomplish. We would also discuss the different meets I was interested in attending. We took special care to plan out the season well so that I would be prepared, and not be overrun or underrun as I approached the Olympic Trials.

I can remember saying to Jim that I was still in shock regarding how things had progressed for me. I realized that Jim had believed in me all along, from the day he saw me run in high school, and he never stopped believing in me in college. He was a coach who was understanding, gave me lots of 400m wisdom, and loved track and field. He allowed me to give input into the workouts and I appreciated being a part of the plan. Jim was also like a father to me in the fact that I could talk with him and trust that he had my best interests in mind. He always gave me great advice. He also told me the truth when I needed to hear it the most. He understood me, he worked with me, and he made me see who I could become. Coach Jim also understood my body during the workouts, knew when he could push me, and knew when to back down so that I would not get injured. We worked well together and we were a great team!

Practices were serious, but we found a way to make them fun. We often would joke at practice and Chris would pretend to be one of my female competitors as we lined up for the reps of the workouts. It always reminded me of who I would be up against at the Olympic Trials. It kept things fun and certainly helped the mood when Coach Jim wanted me to run 3x300 at top end speed or his other favorite workout, repeat split 350s. I dreaded the pain of those workouts, but they made me stronger, faster and a better 400 meter runner. Race modeling during the workouts was helpful for me to mentally prepare and visualize how I would execute my race plan. I pushed myself to the limits in practice. I pushed myself so hard that at times I felt as if I would pass out because of the lactic acid building up. I had gotten really good at visually seeing myself as if I were in a race and being able to perform the way my coach would want me to, and knowing the rhythm of my stride. I would hear Coach Jim's voice calling out my times at practice and it would help me to dig deep as I rounded the bend of the track. The days of work I was putting in at my "oval office" were paying off. I am so thankful and appreciative that I had him in my corner. When you are surrounded by good people, good things happen to you.

As a professional athlete who was sponsored by Nike, I enjoyed coming home to many boxes of gear, shoes and equipment. I was making an income from running and I was excited to have some-thing to show for my hard work and years of dedication. My mom loved hearing my stories of traveling all over the world and was very impressed when I was on TV or in the newspaper. Chris and I would reminisce about the crazy plan I had to quit my job and run professionally. I remember him saying, "What were we thinking? You had been running for four years post collegiately and hadn't made any money. Now, you were just going to quit your job and become a track star? It was a crazy plan, BUT IT WORKED!"

Although I knew I would come back to teaching, it was one of the best decisions I ever made. Being able to completely focus on running, and put all my energy into it certainly helped me make it to the next level. I had a wonderful chiropractor who made sure my body was in line and on point. My massage therapist was able to rub out the knots and flush out the build up from my workouts on a weekly basis. I got serious about eating a balanced diet and tried to limit my intake of processed foods.

During the build up to the Olympic Trials, my mom, Athens, was impressed by all the media attention I was getting. She enjoyed seeing me do interviews and being on the local news in Cincinnati. She was so proud of her daughter. She would call up what seemed to be the whole state of Ohio, and all our family from around the world to tell them about what I was doing. She would remind them to watch me on TV and that I was racing to make the 2008 Olympic Team. It worked out better for Athens to stay home from this Olympic Trials. She was getting older, wasn't able to walk around as much, and would quickly get tired. She didn't mind watching on television, because she knew that she could follow along as if she was there. I could tell that my mom got nervous whenever I ran. She didn't like to show it, but I know she enjoyed screaming at the TV and jumping up and down as best as she could at her age.

The 2008 Olympic Trials were held in Eugene, Oregon, the best place ever to have a track meet! The hospitality of the city of Eugene was a true sight to see. Walking through the airport, I could see USA track and field banners, posters, and signs all over the place. They read, "Welcome. Welcome. Welcome to the 2008 Olympic Trials.

You are here in Eugene, Oregon, to become one of the best and to make the world's hardest team to make." The people were amazing as well. They were so with it. It seemed like everyone knew every single track athlete that was competing in the meet and the vibe was amazing. I knew going into the meet that I had some great competitors and nothing was set in stone. You had to prove yourself or you weren't going to the Olympics. No one had a free pass. Anything could happen. No one was safe from a potential injury or just plain having a bad race when it counted the most. One bad break and you had to wait four more years for your next shot at Olympic glory. I enjoyed the camaraderie among the women of the 400 meters. We were fierce competitors on the track, but friends any other time. When it was show time, it was amazing to see the fierce look on everyone's face. The seriousness, the poise, the look of a diva, and the confidence in our walks. The 400 was a serious matter. I was happy to already have had an Olympic Trials experience four years earlier. It didn't make 2008 seem less nerve wrecking, but at least I knew what to expect. I had been down this road before, only now I was so much more prepared. I headed into the meet feeling excited, ready and eager. I had trust in my coach and I had trust in my training.

My rituals for my meet remained the same. I would lay my uniform out on the bed or chair, nice and neatly so that it would not get messed up. I also wanted to be able to see my uniform and make sure that I did not forget any of the key pieces. Surprisingly our uniforms had multiple pieces to them. It included a running top, buns or boy shorts to match, tights, then jogging pants and a shirt to layer on top. At times, depending on the weather, you would dress up in your warm up jacket too. I then would take my night-before Epsom salt soak and gear my legs up for the races. After soaking, I would visualize what I saw myself doing the next day and I would talk myself through the race. Additionally, my rituals included talking with God and praying.

God had blessed me with this gift and I thanked him daily for that. I thanked him for my coach, for my husband who was my training partner, and for all my family and supporters. My talks with God would vary and in the end I just would ask him to bless my legs and my body to do his will. The morning time would come and it would be show time to gear up for race day. I ate the same breakfast for every competition; oatmeal, one half of a bagel (no cream cheese), a banana, yogurt, apple juice and water. I never deviated from that breakfast of champions. I made sure to also apply my makeup the same way every time I ran in meets. My gold eye shadow was my signature piece. I liked wearing it to show that I was going for the gold. I was ready. I had a different level of confidence and I wasn't afraid. I was going into this meet on a mission and I knew my competitors already so it was GAME TIME. They were going to learn more about who Mary Wineberg was and what she was about.

I vowed to go out and give my all in each round of the women's 400m. I wanted to lay it on the track like there was no tomorrow. I told my agent and coach that I was going to make it to the final. I told them confidently that I was going to aim to make that team. I found out the lane that I would be in for the first round of the women's 400. I tried not to fixate over who was in my heat or make a stink about what lane I was in, but knowing my lane and competitors would help me with my race plan. The first round at the trials went well for me and I won my heat. I did what my coach asked me to do. I got out well, relaxed on the backstretch, starting picking up around the curve and finished strong. I was very proud after that first round, but I knew the semi-final would be more challenging. Your body is tired from the day before and now you are running on back to back days. Regardless of how you feel, you have to convince yourself that you feel great. In a meet like the Olympic Trials, you have to treat the semi-final just like it is the actual final. If you take it for granted, you could get left out of the final. The final includes eight people. I wanted one of those lanes.

The next day came and I was ready. I executed the same race plan from the preliminaries, but pushed even more through the final 100 meters. I won my heat again and had officially made it to the final.

Right after the race, I found my coach and husband. We were all excited, but focused on the next day. I was going to be in the final, running for a spot on the Olympic Team. I was going to do what I had to do to make that team. Lewis Johnson, who was a sports commentator for NBC, came over to talk to me. He was a friend and a fellow Bearcat student athlete. He was an outstanding 800-meter runner at the University of Cincinnati and still holds the school record in the event. He became a well-known rabbit on the international circuit for track and field and that developed into a career as a sports commentator. He was commentating the meet and congratulated me on the race. We were able to have a proud moment and he was excited that he would be able to talk about me the next day in the final.

Back at the hotel, it finally sank in that I was a finalist in the women's 400 meters. I was on top of the world. I thanked Jim and Chris for believing in me and told them that I was going to do something special the next day. I was electrified that things were working out for me. That evening, I got a call on my cell phone from sports commentator, Carol Lewis. She called to do an interview with me and ask my feelings about the race. She wanted to know my game plan and what making the final meant to me. I responded to her that I was excited to be in the race, and I was going to do whatever I needed to do to cross the line to make the team. I wanted to make my mom even more proud of me. As I explained my game plan to Carol, I could feel the butterflies enter my stomach. The next day I had some big expectations to live up to, and I had to be ready to show the crowd my ability. The local Eugene paper, The Register, wrote up a wonderful article on me and what I might accomplish in the race. They had a picture of me on the front page of the newspaper as it highlighted the Olympic

Trials activity and results. The write up was done outstandingly well and it pushed me to come through based on what it said about me.

The day of the final…..

I arrived at the warm-up track, and I felt great. My legs were a little tired and sore, but it wasn't anything I couldn't handle. After my warm up, the officials walked us out to the starting area and I was ready to go. Everyone was focused and in their race mode. As I started to take my warm up clothes off, I looked at the other lanes and said to myself, "I'm going to go for it." I shook out my legs as the starter got into position.

"Runners, on your mark." I tapped my feet into the blocks, and settled into position. This was a do or die situation. I was going to bust out of those blocks as fast as I possibly could. "SET", "BANG" and the gun blasted.

I took off………….

I got out well, but then I totally went against everything that my coach had told me to use as our race plan. I was supposed to relax on the backstretch, but I had gotten too excited. I could feel Sanya on my outside and I pushed the entire backstretch, moving past her and into 1st place. As we came into the curve with 200 meters to go, she made her move and I tried to pick it up even more. With 150m to go, I knew I was in trouble. I had used up too much of my energy on the backstretch. Sanya pulled away and I tried to hold on going into the final 100 meters. I was well ahead of everyone else, but the entire field of runners was closing in on me. With 50 meters to go my body started to tense up, and my arms shrunk up close to my chest. My form fell apart and I started to move in slow motion. "Oh, no!" I thought. What was going to happen? What if I couldn't make it to the line? I was still holding on to second place, but the other runners were inching closer and closer. I didn't know if I was going to make it to the finish line and it felt like everyone was going to pass me. I prayed and said, "God, help me hold on. Please get me to that line."

My body sank lower to the ground, my legs started to buckle with each stride, I leaned forward and crumbled as I crossed the finish line. Four other girls crossed at practically the same time. Had I done it or did my Olympic dream turn into a nightmare? I looked up at the scoreboard and anxiously waited for the times to be displayed. I did it! I held on by the slimmest of margins. I saw my name flash up in 2nd place! I jumped up and screamed at the fact that I had made my first Olympic team. I didn't even care that I had fallen and was scraped up. I was just so excited and lost in the moment. I immediately hugged anyone that was around me. I went over and hugged Sanya, congratulating her on her victory and I hugged DeeDee who came in third, just 3-hundredths (0.03) of a second behind me. I was only 13 hundredths (0.13) from getting passed by another runner which would have pushed me back to 4th and I would have missed out on making the Olympics in the open 400m. Had I run just 0.46 seconds slower, I would have missed out on the Olympics altogether.

It seemed like I had just gotten off the ground and I was being ushered over by the media to be interviewed. I said onto the camera, "I'm just so thankful. I'm just so blessed to have made this team. It's been four long years. Hi Mom," I knew Athens was watching at home. We jogged our victory lap. I waved to the fans of Eugene, Oregon, and was ecstatic that I had made it. I was so thankful. I was going to Beijing. I was now an Olympian. I connected with my coach, Chris, and his parents and we all rejoiced together. There were several other UC Bearcats competing in the meet and they came over to congratulate me as well. It was nice to have my mother- and father-in-law there to share the moment with me. I gave Chris and Coach Jim the biggest hugs, and I could tell by the look on Chris' face that he was in shock. He said to me, "You scared me to death. I thought you didn't make it. I thought you were passed at the line when you fell." I looked at him and said, "Oh well, I made it".

Although I didn't run according to my race plan, I was so thankful that I was able to hold on through the line. I had trained and prepared so well, that having an off race did not even keep me from my Olympic dream. It also gave me great pleasure to see my friend, and former Bearcats teammate, David Payne, make the Olympic team in the 110 hurdles. We both would be representing Cincinnati and the Bearcats at the Olympic Games.

# ELEVEN

# The Olympic Games

On the day of our 2nd wedding anniversary, August 5th, 2008, we traveled to China for the Olympic Games. I arrived ten days before the start of the Olympics. The USA coaching staff wanted all athletes to get acclimated to the time change and rest up from the travel well before we would need to compete. In Beijing, I was in awe of the entire Olympic experience. The Olympic Village where I stayed was an exciting place immersed in Olympic athletes from all over the world. All of the facilities were brand new and my walk into the "Bird's Nest" track and field stadium for the first time was mesmerizing. It was massive and seated over 90,000 people.

My experience running the open 400 meters was not quite what I was expecting or looking for. I made it through the preliminaries and into the semi-final, but I didn't feel great and was battling a bit of sore hamstring. I felt off in the semi-final and did not advance to the final. Was this going to be my Olympic experience? Did I do enough to impress the coaching staff to still run me on the 4x400 relay coming up in a few days? I needed to get myself together and stay focused despite the overwhelming environment. I took a day to do some sightseeing and tried to take my mind off the meet and my disappointment in the open 400m. I toured the Great Wall of China and visited Tiananmen Square. The next day I focused on recovery and rehab and tried to get my body and mind feeling good again. I started to bounce back and look forward to the opportunity I still had in front of me. I was told I would be running the preliminary round of the 4x400 relay and that we needed to get the stick around the track cleanly to get into the final which was held the day after the prelim. They selected me to lead off and I was once again on a mission. I ran a strong leg and started to feel like myself again. I positioned the USA team into 1st place, and the rest of the girls ran well, earning us a spot in the final the following night.

This is where the mental struggle really began. The coaches told me I did a good job, but they didn't say anything about if I would be on the final team the next day. They said we would have a meeting the next day to go over who would run. My mind started racing in all directions…"Did I do enough for them to run me on the final? I didn't run that well in the prelims of the open 400 so they might not run me. But then, they would surely run me, I placed 2nd at the trials. Did they already tell the other girls who would actually be running?" I had to battle with my own thoughts through the night and into the next day until our meeting. It was agonizing. I had friends and family telling me that they would be watching and I didn't even know if I would be running. The meeting could not come quick enough. We all entered the room and anxiously sat down. The coach started to speak, "This is the order for the final. Wineberg, Felix, Henderson, Richards." Hallelujah, praise the Lord! I leapt on the inside, but kept my composure. My fire was back and I was ready for the race that night! It would surely be a battle, a clash of the titans between the United States, Russia, Jamaica, and Great Britain. Russia had placed three women in the 400m final. Jamaica had placed two in the final and Great Britain had the 400 meter Olympic Champion.

We traveled to the stadium from the Olympic village and it was complete silence on the bus, except for some faint sounds escaping from each girl's headphones. We were in meet mode and focused like never before. Our warm up went well and we headed into the Olympic Stadium on the final night of all competition. The stadium was absolutely packed and you couldn't escape the intensity of the moment. I walked out to my blocks as the camera was in my face and I looked around at the other lanes. OH MY GOODNESS! The other teams were coming out swinging, each popping off their best runner! Great Britain was leading off the Olympic champion, Christine Ohuruogu. Jamaica was leading off the silver medalist, Novlene Williams, and Russia was leading off the 4th place finisher from open 400. We were saving our only finalist for the anchor leg and here I was basically thrown into a rematch of the Olympic 400 meter final. As I started to set my blocks my nerves took over. Which leg do I have forward? I asked myself. Which hand do I hold the baton with? I needed to get it together and get it together quick. I tuned everything out and reminded myself of how I did it just last night. I got dialed in and got everything squared away. I was ready and had my game face on.

"On your marks," said the starter. Over 90,000 fans instantly became silent and over a billion people were tuned in on TV. The gun went off and I powered out of the blocks. I pushed the first curve and then relaxed on the backstretch. It looked as if I lost some ground, but I needed to execute my race. I started working the final curve, making some ground back up on my opponents. I felt great and blistered down the final homestretch, handing off to Allyson Felix tied for first. In the American television broadcast, Ato Bolden commentated, "But Mary Wineberg did her part. She has handed off to Allyson Felix just about even in first."

Allyson raced around the first curve and battled with Jamaica on the backstretch to establish our position as the first place team. She pushed the curve and finished strong, extending the lead as she handed off to our 3rd leg, Monique Henderson. Monique ran fast through the first 200 meters, but Russia was closing in around the final curve.

Russia overtook the United States down the homestretch and handed off to the anchor leg in first place. Russia held the lead around the first curve and started to extend the lead on the backstretch. Sanya Richards starting narrowing the gap around the final curve, but would it be too late? Both athletes kicked down the homestretch, Russia held the lead, but with 50 meters to go, Sanya started to close in even more. They battled stride for stride until the final steps of the race. Russia started to break down and Sanya Richards prevailed for the United States crossing the line in first, securing Olympic Gold, and running one of the fastest times in the history of the World! We all rushed out to embrace in a hug and we said a prayer together. We did it. We really did it! My hopes, my dreams, my hard work, my tears, my years of struggle, my ups, my downs, my unwavering perseverance all came together in perfect unison, and what was once seemed like a scattered series of random events, aligned in an instant, and made complete and perfect sense.

# TWELVE

## A New Addition

After winning my gold medal and coming back to Cincinnati, I enjoyed all the events, honors and celebrations that were put on for me. It was amazing to see how many fans I had in the city and how many people supported and cheered me on. It was encouraging to hear the stories of so many women, kids, and men that I had inspired. I was taken aback by all of the overwhelming gratitude people expressed and to hear from so many people that I was a role model or a hero. I was a proud member of TEAM USA. I was an Olympic Gold Medalist. I was the University of Cincinnati's first female athlete to have medaled at an Olympic Games in track and field, and I was the first African American female from the University of Cincinnati and Walnut Hills to have medaled from track and field in the Olympics. People were mentioning my name. I was proud to be named to the University of Cincinnati famous graduates list and to be among people such as the great Oscar Robertson. Oscar was a UC grad and a basketball legend. I had not even begun to understand the depth of what I had just accomplished.

Chris and I had always wanted to start a family, but due to my obligations of being a professional athlete, it wasn't something that I could easily do. I had to think about if it was the right time and how would it affect my track career. I wondered how quickly I could come back? I then realized that it didn't matter, because I had fulfilled my destiny. I would be content if I never raced again. I enjoyed running and made a commitment to make a comeback, but growing a family was my priority. We both agreed that it was TIME for our family to expand. Truth be told, I wasn't getting any younger and I had the true itch for a baby. In October, Chris and I found out that I was indeed pregnant. We jumped for joy and screamed, "We're having a baby!"

We told our family and they too were very excited for us. My mom was going to be a grandmother and she was so ecstatic. This would be her first grandchild. Finding out that I was pregnant was the best thing that could have happened to us at that time. Weeks later, it sunk in that I would indeed have to take a year off. We had already let my coach know I was pregnant and he enjoyed hearing the big news. I told Chris that I would reach out to my sponsors and agent. I had just been up for negotiations at the end of the season with my Nike contract. I was told they renewed my contract and increased my base salary. I wanted to be honest with my sponsor so my agent made the call to my Nike rep to let them know the news. Things were great. I was doing speaking events all over the city and continued to be honored for my accomplishments. A month or two went by and I realized that I had not received my quarterly check from Nike. When I inquired, I was informed that my contract was never put through legal and I had been released as a Nike athlete. I was devastated and shocked that they would do this. I had a few conversations with my Nike contact and they didn't budge. They said that I was an independent contractor and I could not perform the duties they had previously hired me to do. I decided to let it go, move on and not get bitter. My husband and I had been smart with my earnings and we would be financially stable with or without Nike.

It was a very different feeling to have a life growing inside of me. The different monthly changes that occurred were both educational and interesting. We took it upon ourselves and continued to have me train every day, just with slight modifications. My coach and doctor were on board. I actually still competed during the first part of my pregnancy, up until about five months. I remember running an indoor meet at Indiana University, and not really telling anyone that I was pregnant. I was pretty nervous about it. "Wow, I have never raced with a baby inside of me; I wonder how this is going to feel?"

I ended up winning the 400 meter race and my competitors were quite shocked when they found out after the race that a pregnant girl had beaten them. I decided to just take it easy for the rest of the pregnancy. I still ran here and there for fun, but for the most part I enjoyed pregnancy. Chris was a great husband. Whatever I needed during these months, he was right there to provide it. My craving was strawberry water. I needed it and had to have it. I wanted strawberries, fresh strawberries cut up in water. Sometimes I asked for it at 1:00 in the morning and Chris would get up to make me my special water and strawberry mix. When I think about it, he probably deserved husband of the year for how he cared for this pregnant and emotional lady. As the months moved on and my stomach grew, I was ready to have this child. I can remember the doctor saying that there was a possibility that she might be late and I just kept thinking that she'd better come early. I knew that I wanted this lovely little girl out of my stomach and I wanted her in this world so I could hold her. We had previously come up with a list of names that we both liked. It was hard to choose, but eventually we selected Brooklyn. I think the deciding factor was that it paid homage to me being born in Brooklyn, New York.

On August the 3rd, 2009 Brooklyn Marie Wineberg was born and entered into the world with such a very loud cry. It was such a beautiful blessing. Holding her in my arms for the first time was the most wonderful experience. I was speechless at first and then the words, "Babe, she's beautiful," trembled out of my mouth. As I held her close in my arms, I realized that my most important title was not Olympic Gold Medalist anymore. It was Mom. I had welcomed a life into this world and I prayed that God would make me the best mom that I could be. I prayed that he would provide me with the skills to teach her and guide her. I had been a role model to many, but now this baby would grow up and look to me for everything. I didn't want to let her down and I didn't want her to experience what I had gone through. I knew Chris would be an excellent father and would do a great job of playing with her, teaching her, and always being there for her. On the day of our 3rd wedding anniversary, August 5th, 2009, we brought our first child home from the hospital.

Caring for her, changing diapers, staying up late, waking up early, and feedings in the middle of the night was challenging, but it was so worth it. It was a lot to adjust to, but we did it. We had a plan in place and we figured out who would take the different shifts. I was starting to miss running and was ready to go back to training. I was ready to return to the oval office. I was cleared by my doctor; she was so supportive of my career and made sure I was healed. I was ready to go after the 2010 season. I will admit, training was very difficult at first. It was very hard trying to get back into shape. My whole body felt so weak. My doctor explained that right after you have a child, your ligaments and everything are still so loose and stretchy, and it would take a while for everything to tighten back up. I had to be very careful that I didn't injure myself. I had to be very careful that I wasn't rushing back too soon.

My first month back at the track gave me a huge wake up call. It was as if I was starting all over again. I had done some research and learned that sometimes when a female athlete has a child, they come back stronger and have a surge in ability. Well, I must have missed that boat, because I was struggling and I was struggling badly. Honestly, I didn't feel the same. I struggled even hitting the easiest times my coach wanted me to run. Was it time for me to call it quits?

I decided not to quit. I pushed through the pain and fought against all the doubts that told me I couldn't do this. I very slowly felt the shape coming back and started to feel like my old self again. The 2010 season went okay. I got my time back down to 52.29 and competed at USA Nationals, but I certainly needed to improve in the coming seasons to have a shot at the 2012 Olympic Games. I had two years to train. I saw improvements in 2011 and got back down into the 51s. During those seasons, I enjoyed having Chris and Brooklyn travel with me. I was thankful that Brooklyn was able to travel and see so many places, even if she was too young to remember. As Brooklyn got older she started to learn about the sport and she knew that her mom had won a gold medal. I could tell that she thought it was cool to be able to get on airplanes, meet some of mommy's athlete friends, and be able to cheer and say, "Go Mom!" I really enjoyed having that experience with her. She made me want to be better and helped me persevere. I didn't have a shoe sponsor for quite some time. The shoe companies that gave out contracts wanted up-and-coming athletes. They wanted athletes to be injury free and on their A game. Then I was stricken by an injury and was losing hope. I prayed and continued to ask God for guidance. One day my agent contacted me with some awesome news. He had found a sponsor interested in working with me. I was so proud to be sponsored by Brooks and to be able to wear the NYAC uniform. The New York Athletic Club believed in me and I admired the foot emblem that graced their uniforms. I could not have asked for better sponsors, they were amazing and so supportive during this time. They gave me an opportunity, they gave me a chance.

I entered the 2012 season with a lot of positive energy. It was the Olympic year and I was looking forward to the Olympic trials.

Leading into the trials, I didn't feel 100% at my best, but I knew that anything could happen. I had been praying. I had been talking to God. I had been writing down my goals. The Olympic Trials were back in Eugene, Oregon. The atmosphere and environment brought back so many memories of the 2008 trials. It was very nostalgic for me to compete at Hayward Field in an Olympic Trials once again. The jitters and the nerves were there, but it wasn't quite the same as in 2008. I had a lower level of nervousness. To me, as an athlete, you want those nerves and those butterflies. It means you care and overcoming them gives you a positive energy that you can turn into faster times.

I ran well in the prelims, easily advancing into the semi-final. In the semi-final I ran tough, but came up one place short of making the final. It was a hard pill to swallow, but things happen for a reason.

# THIRTEEN

## Losing a Mother's Love

I came back home to Cincinnati and I was fine. I was okay with what had happened and I thought it was probably time to wrap up my career. I had lived out my dreams and I had fulfilled my commitment to making a comeback to the sport after having child. I was satisfied having a gold medal from both an Olympic Games and a World Championship. I was grateful that throughout my career I had been able to travel to so many different places. I had met so many wonderful people and I had made so many friends.

My mom was proud of me, despite my not making the team this time. Her health had been deteriorating. Not only did she have diabetes, but she was on dialysis as well. We had actually helped her to buy a house just across the street from our home so I could help her out and check on her regularly. I was checking on her several times a day at this point. I took her out to the movies for her 82nd birthday and we had a great time. A few days later, I was scheduled to take her to a morning doctor's appointment. I called to make sure she was up and ready, but she didn't answer the phone. After a couple attempts, I walked over to check on her and what I had always feared was exactly what I found. She had gotten up that morning, but something in her deteriorating body finally gave way.

I lost my mom. I lost my friend. I lost the person who I looked up to, and who gave me a chance in this world. Now, I was dealing with death for a second time. Yes, throughout my years I had people die and people pass away, but it was now my mom. The one who cared for me and adopted me. She was gone. There was nothing that I could do. There was nothing that would bring her back. She had suffered a stroke. I realized then why I did not make that Olympic team. I would have been in another country trying to prepare for the Olympic Games. I would have had to rush back and would have missed competing anyway. I would have missed out on her birthday and I wouldn't have been there to spend some of the very last moments with her that I could cherish and that truly mattered to me.

I was heartbroken. I was sad. I was hurt. I was lonely. I didn't want to talk to anyone. I cried continuously for days and I wanted to curl up into a ball and sleep the pain away. I wanted to ask, "Why, God? Why did you have to take her away from me?" I was very thankful that my husband was there for support during this very emotional time. He didn't know what to say to comfort me but he knew being there for me was more than enough. All I could cry out and say to him is that I wanted my mom back. I wanted her to be able to see Brooklyn one more time. I wanted to be able to hear her voice.

I realized that she was in a better place. I realized that she had lived her life to the fullest and I mean the fullest. She was no longer in pain. I was happy that I was able to have her live across the street from me. I saw her every single day. I spent hours and hours with her. She was able to see me become a mom and was able to share the joy in spending time with Brooklyn as she grew into a little girl.

Yes, it took months for me to get over her death, not because I was angry. But it took so much because I had also been her caregiver. I had been the person that she depended on, and I depended on her. I helped her daily with just her regular routines. I prepared her for dialysis treatments, cared for her and was there to talk if she needed. I had this empty feeling in the fact that I wouldn't be hearing her voice anymore. I wouldn't be seeing her lovely face. I wouldn't be hearing her jokes, and I wouldn't be able to have her come over to the house anymore. Those were the things that I was going to miss the most. I had to realize that we don't live forever. She was a wise woman. She taught me so much. She taught me how to live a purposeful life and she reminded me that we all must leave the Earth at some point. When you loose someone suddenly, often times you wish you could say this or do that. I was so happy that I knew that I had done my best and she appreciated me. If she were here today, I would say, "Mom, you are an amazing woman, and I thank you so much for loving me. I thank you for caring for me. I thank you for raising me. I thank you for giving me joy every day. I thank you for giving me discipline. I thank you for giving me rules. I thank you for trusting me. I thank you for allowing me to live my life. I thank you for being the best mother that you could possibly be to me and I love you."

Even though I thought I was done running, I decided to run another year and dedicate it to my mom. She had loved watching me run and started to appreciate and follow the sport. In 2013, in every single race, I ran with a guardian angel pin attached to my uniform in remembrance of her. It was she that was with me every day on the track at practice. It was she who was with me every day. She made me tell myself after waking up that I was going to just give my best. It was she that was with me when I attended the meets. It was she who was with me when I stepped into the blocks. The 2013 season started off very well for me. I was on fire during the indoor season and had won every single meet I competed in. I won the New Balance Games and the prestigious Milrose Games. I had set a new indoor personal record in the 400 meters for the first time since 2008. My sponsor, the New York Athletic Club, featured me on the cover of their magazine and I was very honored to represent them.

I was feeling great and was actually the favorite to win the indoor National title. Unfortunately, I got tangled up with the other runners trying to win the break in the final and I ended up falling and not being able to finish the race. I brushed off the disappointment and got focused for the outdoor season. That outdoor season I ran the fastest time I had run since 2008. I missed out on making the outdoor World Championship team, but was able to finish my career with three straight victories at international competitions. I was finally ready to hang up my spikes for good. I was ready to move on to a new chapter in my life. I knew my mom was proud of me. I knew that Chris was proud of me. I knew that Brooklyn was proud of me, but most of all, I was proud of myself.

# FOUTEEN

## Finding Her

Having lost the woman I called mom and the one who had served as my mom, it made me think about my birth mother. I'd always had questions, but now I really wanted some answers about her. Was she still alive? What was she doing? Does she ever think about me? Does she remember me? Is she looking for me? Do I have any brothers or sisters? Does she know what I have done with my life? Does she know that I went on to get a college degree, win an Olympic Gold Medal, and have a baby of my own?

I would occasionally browse through public records to see if I could find anything on her. I called the Social Security office to see if there was any record of her death. I thought about hiring an investigator. I would see talk show episodes on TV of people being reunited with lost family members and I wondered if I should try to contact Oprah or something. I Googled my birth mother's name from time to time to see if anything would pop up. One day, I was browsing on Facebook and I decided to search for her last name. I wondered if she still lived in New York so I started combing through profiles with her last name that were in New York. I reached out to some of them and started to put things together. I finally found and messaged someone, asking if they knew of a relative of mine. I stated her name.

The response I received back made me nearly pass out, "Yeah, that's your mom. I know where she is and I can give you a number to get in touch with her."

I literally jumped out of my seat. I got very nervous, I got very jittery, and I did not know what to do. Did I really want to do this? They sent me the number, but I hid it away and didn't call it. About a week went by and I couldn't shake my yearning to learn more. I pulled the number back out and gave it a call.

I can't remember how I started the conversation, but my birth mother was in shock and so excited to hear my voice, I heard all the words I had hoped to hear. "I love you. I miss you. I didn't know where you were. I did everything to try to find you. I have been looking all over for you."

I was so excited and felt the most amazing joy. We talked for hours. I woke up the next day feeling great. It wasn't until I started going over our conversation in my head that I realized something wasn't right. This wasn't adding up. It didn't make sense. I remembered the broken promises to come see me. I remembered Athens telling her where we were and that she could always call the operator and ask for the number. *How could you have done everything to try to find me, yet you never found me?* I lived in the same house in Cincinnati until I was an adult. I was deemed a ward of the state when they couldn't find you. Where had she been looking for me at? I desperately wanted to ignore these thoughts and go back to the night before. I even tried to push the thoughts out and hold on to her words as truth. I tried to convince myself that maybe I didn't remember some of the things from my childhood accurately and she was telling the truth. I so wanted to live in the fairytale world she had described that she didn't know where I was, and had frantically been searching for me. But I had to come back to reality. I couldn't come to grips with it at first, but being a mother myself I couldn't relate. How do you not know where your daughter is? How do you not know the phone number of where she is? How do you lose track of your daughter? I would never lose track of my daughter. I realized that sometimes a person's perception is not reality. Sometimes a reality can be so painful that your mind changes facts and reorganizes events and fashions a situation into something you can handle. I had to process that what I had wanted to hear for over thirty years and after all that waiting, I finally heard, only to suddenly realize that it wasn't real.

I did believe some of it was real. I believed she missed me at times. I believed she loved me in a way that she understands love. I don't think it was easy for her to see that she couldn't care for me at that time. Perhaps she had some sleepless nights and I know I wasn't forgotten. I think she felt guilt. I think she felt shame and had told people for so long that she'd tried hard to find me that she started to believe it herself. We continued to speak over the next few months and tried to somehow develop a relationship. I decided that I was ready to meet her. I wanted to meet the woman who gave me birth and meet the other side of my family. Chris and I traveled to New York without telling her the date I was coming. I had butterflies in my stomach. I was antsy. I was nervous because I didn't know what to expect. What would it actually be like to see her in person? I prayed about it and I prayed about it. I asked God to give me strength and to allow for healing. I had realized that I had not forgiven her. I didn't necessarily hold a grudge, but I hadn't completely let my pain go. . I informed a cousin I would be coming and she arranged to have my birth mother there waiting. I walked through the doorway and I saw my birth mother for the first time in over thirty years. She was shocked and absolutely thrilled to see me. There were tears. There was joy. There were more tears. There were hugs and screams. I was excited, and I was happy that I made the trip. I could tell that she was very excited and sincerely thankful to have me in her arms once again. She held me so tight and she didn't want to let me go. It was a bittersweet feeling, but one I desperately needed. A calmness came over me, and there was a feeling of closure I thought would forever be missing in my life.

# REFLECTION

## Making Peace with it All

Coming home after that visit and over the year, I took it day by day with my birth mother. There was still hurt, pain, distance and just really getting to know each other. I had forgiven her and I realized that I had to let the animosity go and release it. What becomes of us, only time will tell? I had found my answers and I now knew where I came from. Again day by day……..

Now that I was experiencing personal growth, I wanted to pursue a different career path. I wanted to do something that would make me happy and allow me to make an imprint on other's lives. After retiring from the sport of track and field, I was ready to get serious about my passion to be an educator. I had always loved teaching and being a role model to our youth. I went back to school and earned my master's degree in early childhood education. At the same time, the baby itch was back and Chris and I were ready to grow our family even more. I quickly became pregnant and everything was going according to plan. I felt great. I was excited about my new direction in life and I was excited to have another baby. Despite being retired from running, I desired to still be involved with USA Track and Field to help the sport. I attended the annual meeting convention in 2014, but did not tell anyone I was pregnant. I was glowing and some even mentioned it to me while in Indianapolis. It was so hard not to share my secret with some of my track family that I was surrounded by. But I'm thankful I kept the news to myself, because then tragedy hit. The day after I returned home from the annual meeting convention, I woke up with a pain in my stomach and a terrible feeling in my heart. I had suffered a miscarriage. It caught me completely by surprise. I was devastated. I was saddened. The first pregnancy went so well. I never expected this. I wondered why and realized that sometimes we just don't know why. I told myself that I was afraid to try again but, after talking with my doctor, she assured me that sometimes it just happens. I wanted to be hopeful.

We decided to try again several months later. I became pregnant and at the same time was hired as a 2nd grade teacher in Cincinnati Public Schools. Throughout the pregnancy, I was very nervous. What if I miscarry again? What if....? I didn't know if I would have the courage to try again if this pregnancy didn't work out. Praise God, things went smoothly and on January the 13th, 2015 Olivia Christine Wineberg was born. She too was such a beautiful sight. We now had two wonderful girls. I was so thankful and thanked God every day for my two beautiful girls. They absolutely mean the world to me. They bring such joy and pleasure to our lives and make us better. I want to be the best example to them of what a strong woman looks like, acts like and ultimately what they too can become. I want them to know LOVE, and see that their parents think the world of them.

Through connecting with my birth mother, I was able to finally forgive her and find PEACE. It was the hardest thing to do and I have no problem admitting that. A burden was lifted off my chest and I can say that it was therapeutic. It allowed me to let the past be the past and realize that we can only move forward. I was able to explain to her my hurt and my pain. And I was able to see her hurt and pain as well. I was able to see her for her. This is a process, a never ending process. It will continue to take time and I hope for the best as we both continue to heal.

"If you cannot find peace within yourself,
you will never find it anywhere else."
-Marvin Gaye

# Gratitude

I would like to thank everyone who was instrumental in encouraging me to write and share my story. You reminded me on why it is that I have a story to tell. I am proud and humbled to be surrounded by such inspirational stories and accomplishments. You all will never know just how much I appreciated your daily words, text messages and calls that pushed me in the right direction. I spent many years going back and forth on if I could do this. I said that once I was done that it would be worth it. I am so elated that I did! I have such a huge support team in my corner and I am thankful for my family, and friends.

Chris, you are my biggest supporter, my backbone, my husband, and my best friend. Thank you for always being by my side through everything. I could not of done this without you. Your unwavering love is what I admire about you. I hope that our daughters will find this same type of love in their future. I love and appreciate you, thank you again from the bottom of my heart.

Brooklyn and Olivia thank you for being such wonderful daughters. I hope as you get older that you will be able to know the true meaning of this story and all that it entails. I hope to inspire you! May you reach for your dreams and know that you can be anything in this world. I love you both and your future is BRIGHT.

Through the years as a motivational speaker I have reached many individuals and the feedback I got was that I inspire them, and I allow others to see that they can reach their dreams. I want you all to see your dreams and go for them. I want you to seek out closure if you are in pain. I want you to be your BEST. Make the most of your opportunity, and I challenge you to find peace within yourself. I challenge you to have faith, to have determination and to demonstrate UNWAVERING PERSEVERANCE~~~~

# Photos

**My kindergarten picture age 5**

Me at a young age with Athens in Cincinnati

Senior yearbook photo-Walnut Hills

2001 College Track (University of Cincinnati) &
2003 Indoor World's-Moscow

My wedding day with my mom and realizing
that I was all grown up now

**Practicing with Chris my training partner and husband**

**Enjoying the moment with Coach Jim and
my husband Chris after making the Olympic Team**

**Running the open 400 meters at the 2008 Olympic Games**

**Passing the baton to Allyson Felix in the
4x400 meter relay at the 2008 Olympics**

**Celebrating Olympic Gold with my teammates**

**Post-Olympic celebration with my coach Jim Schnur**

Cincinnati Magazine
Photoshoot- photo credit Jonathan Robert Willis

**Glowing with expectancy as I await the arrival
of my first child-2009
Photo credit- Lamar Pacley**

Me and my mom, Athens at my University of Cincinnati Hall
of Fame Induction-2010

Honored to represent the New York Athletic Club
at the 2012 Olympic Trials

**Reuniting with my birth mother after 31 years**

Embracing my sorority as I reminiscence on its values,
the sisterhood, my experiences and the service to all mankind.
AKA will forever be a part of me.

Taking my girls back to my high school
to see where it started for me

Family portrait with Chris, Brooklyn and Olivia

Through them I have learned to appreciate and value family more
than ever; the Wineberg's take over